Praise for *Karamo*

"This soul-soothing memoir from one-fifth of the Fab Five (and staunch advocate for LGBTQ mental health awareness) is also a deeply profound rumination on the relationship between one's culture—including what that even means—and one's self-perception."

—OprahMag.com

"During every episode of *Queer Eye*, there's at least one touching moment where Karamo Brown drops some serious wisdom about self-love and makes everybody cry. His moving memoir about overcoming adversity captures that feeling in book form."

—*HelloGiggles*

"*Queer Eye*'s cultural expert Karamo Brown tells his life story—and gives fans a delicious behind-the-scenes look at the taping of the feel-good Netflix series—in his new memoir."

—*Bustle*

"Truly, truly fascinating."

—Trevor Noah on *The Daily Show*

"Brown is candid and warm in all the ways his fans will expect. He relates a childhood filled with both love and trauma, his journey through anger problems and addiction, the stops and starts in creating a career that fit, and his unexpected path to fatherhood. Even his story's happy ending, a hit show and an upcoming wedding, is addressed with introspection. Brown states his passion for helping others find the language to communicate their emotions; readers will appreciate his openheartedness in sharing his own."

—*Booklist*

"A powerful story of a young, gay black man's fight to gain self-empowerment and healing."

—*Publishers Weekly*

"Fans will flock to this sincere memoir and its thoughtful advice."

—*Library Journal*

KARAMO

My Story of Embracing Purpose, Healing, and Hope

Karamo Brown

with Jancee Dunn

Gallery Books

New York   London   Toronto   Sydney   New Delhi

Gallery Books
An Imprint of Simon & Schuster, Inc.
1230 Avenue of the Americas
New York, NY 10020

First Gallery Books trade paperback edition February 2020

GALLERY BOOKS and colophon are registered trademarks of Simon & Schuster, Inc.

For information about special discounts for bulk purchases,
please contact Simon & Schuster Special Sales at 1-866-506-1949
or business@simonandschuster.com.

The Simon & Schuster Speakers Bureau can bring authors to your live event.
For more information or to book an event, contact the Simon & Schuster Speakers
Bureau at 1-866-248-3049 or visit our website at www.simonspeakers.com.

Interior design by Davina Mock-Maniscalco

Manufactured in the United States of America

10   9   8   7   6   5   4   3   2   1

Library of Congress Cataloging-in-Publication Data is available for the hardcover edition.

ISBN 978-1-9821-1197-7
ISBN 978-1-9821-1198-4 (pbk)
ISBN 978-1-9821-1199-1 (ebook)

I dedicate this book
to those who have taught me the greatest lessons—
my father, mother, grandmother, sisters, and friends.
You are the reason I have had both happy and sad tears,
which I have used to water the seeds of growth within myself.

I also want to dedicate this
to all my friends worldwide—those I know personally
and those who know me through my work.
I believe in you, I see you, and I want you to know
that you have the power to create the life you want.

Remember, friends,
we all have inherent value
and you are designed perfectly.

contents

Contents

KARAMO

introduction

As the resident culture expert, therapist, or life coach on *Queer Eye* (you can decide what you want to call me), I help people evaluate how they respond to their internal and external struggles. While my *Queer Eye* castmates make over the contestants' style, home decor, diet, and grooming, my job is to make over their hearts and minds—which is why I love being on the show.

As I write this from the set of *Queer Eye* in Kansas City, Missouri, I have just had a long but rewarding week helping a hero (that's what we call the guests on the show) who was struggling with forgiveness and needing closure. It was my first time exploring this theme this season, and I was very excited about it. I'd spent almost every night coming up with the most impactful ways of helping this hero get to a space where he understood that getting closure from the trauma that had happened in his life began with forgiving himself, then forgiving the person who inflicted the trauma, and, last, accepting that this experience was meant to provide him with a lesson so he could be the amazing person he was destined to be.

Earlier today, my *Queer Eye* castmate Bobby Berk walked into the trailer that the cast uses when we're on set. He stood over me as I sat at my computer and read what I was planning to do with the hero in order to help him get to a place of forgiveness and closure. (To be honest, I like when my castmates, especially Bobby, take a sneak peek at my plans.) Before I could say anything, I felt a small drop of water hit my hand. I turned around and saw that Bobby had tears in his eyes.

"Damn you, Kar-Oprah," he said (that's his nickname for me). "Now you're making me cry, just reading what you're going to be doin'." I laughed, but his response told me I had figured out an effective way to help our hero grow and roll smoothly into his destiny.

(Side note: I wish I could tell you which hero I'm talking about, but contractually I'm not able to write about that person. But once season 3 drops, I wonder if you'll be able to guess who it is.)

Even as I write about this powerful moment, I'm reminded of all the other ones that have happened in these past months. In February of 2018, *Queer Eye* began streaming on Netflix. In less than a year, the boys and I had been to London, Australia, and Japan for the show. We were invited to the Emmys, presented an award—and won three of them. But the most fulfilling thing has been impacting the lives of our heroes and our viewers at home.

Each of us has pulled from not only our training to help people, but also our own personal lives. I'm on *Queer Eye* because I have learned how to manage conflict, both internally and externally. I have had many ups and some major downs that have almost broken me at points—but ultimately, they have made me the man I am. I wasn't always on this path. My journey has included identity confusion, physical and emotional abuse, addiction, violence, and a suicide attempt.

———

I was born in Houston, Texas, in November 1980 to immigrant parents. They had moved to this country from Jamaica to create the life they desired for their children and for themselves—a life full of love, hard work, opportunity, and empathy for others. All their children would go on to attend college, have highly respected professional careers, and find love with amazing partners. I know it was their dream, but to see it actually happen has to have blown their minds. And to see their baby, their only son, go on to build a successful career in television and to be on the Emmys stage winning awards? Now that, I'm sure, they couldn't have imagined.

But it took years of really evaluating my own life for me to understand how to find purpose, healing, and hope within the conflicts that have riddled my life. I've had to overcome many obstacles. And along the way, I have learned that to have a healthy life, you must acknowledge tensions or disagreements—not avoid them. Each moment in my life that I viewed as horrible or hurtful at the time was actually a message that I needed to receive, learn from, and use to inspire others.

I've failed plenty of times as well. But as my granny, Sybil—yes, the one I quote on *Queer Eye* all the time—used to say, "Failure isn't the opposite of success, it's part of it." In this book, I'm going to share intimate stories from my own life in order to show you how I respond to conflict—in hopes that it will inspire a change in you and allow you to get closer to your authentic self. Growth is a journey, not a destination.

———

To truly embrace purpose, healing, and hope in your own life, having the proper language to put your feelings into words is crucial.

Emotions do not happen in response to events, they happen in response to our *thoughts* around that event. Having the vocabulary to name your emotions helps you to see how the way you're thinking is creating them.

When I mastered identifying my feelings, I recognized their

temporary nature—which freed me from much suffering and gave me clarity so I could grow through my conflicts.

By the end of this book, you'll have gained a better understanding of how to use the proper language to communicate with yourself and others by seeing conflict as a springboard to a better you.

If I can find purpose, healing, and hope, then trust me—you can, too. I'm confident that the stories I share of trauma and growth can be a compass for you to find your way toward the life you want and deserve.

chapter one

What's in a Name?

I am my father's only son, and his first boy after having three girls. When my father found out he was having a son, he became a renewed man. He has told me that it made him feel as if he had a chance to do everything right that he felt he hadn't done right before.

During my mother's pregnancy with me, my father became more involved with the Rastafarian faith—learning from his Rastafarian mentor about African heritage and the meaning of names. My father never liked his own name, Henry, so he's always gone by the nickname "Lucky." I'm not sure why he never liked his given name, but as I understand it, he wanted a name for me that reflected and honored our cultural heritage and identity, and not one passed down by British colonizers through slavery.

My mother, my father, Nedra, and Kamilah in 1980. I'm in my mom's belly.

Before I was born, my father became obsessed with learning about the power of one's given name. He read many books on why names are so important in many African cultures. A name is not only your identity, it's the legacy of the people who came before you, and the hope of what you can do with your life. He was convinced that giving me a strong name was the first gift that he could give to me, so he got a book from a Jamaican store in Houston and highlighted his favorites.

Ironically, this gift was also the first act that would cause conflict in my life. Before I was born, he and my mother often fought because they could not agree on my name. I've heard this story many times—my mother didn't want to give me an African name, but my father was adamant. He believed that the name you gave your child affected how they walked through this world, and how they were received.

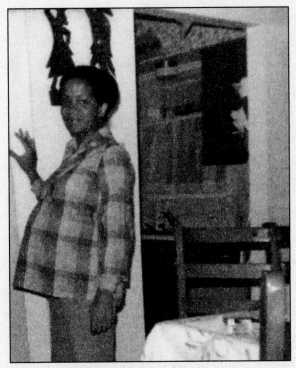

My mother, pregnant with me.

My father went through many, many African names, which caused my parents to have many, many arguments. My mother, Charmaine, who was brought up in a traditional, affluent home in Jamaica, would say, "I'm not giving my son a name that people can't pronounce and that people will think is different. It's 'bad enough' that we're immigrants from Jamaica, and now you're going to put even more pressure on our child." My mother's thinking came from her own mother. My granny Sybil would say, "We're a certain type of black." Constantly, she would say, "We're a different type of black; we're not *those* black folks. We have education; we have money." So in my mother's mind at that time, my name should reflect us being "better" than others.

But my father was stubborn and didn't believe in the ideology of self-worth based on money. He just kept saying, "There's no other option. He has to have a name with meaning. . . . The world is going to know his name, and it must have power."

He eventually settled on Karamo Karega—maybe a month before I was born. Being a charmer, he convinced everyone around him that it was the best name on earth. Eventually, my mother agreed it was a great name. And even my granny, who was against a Rastafarian-inspired name from the beginning, soon told my father, "Oh my gosh, this name is phenomenal."

The name Karamo Karega is Swahili in origin. Karamo means "educated," and Karega means "rebel." My father thought there needed to be a complementing contrast to the meaning of my

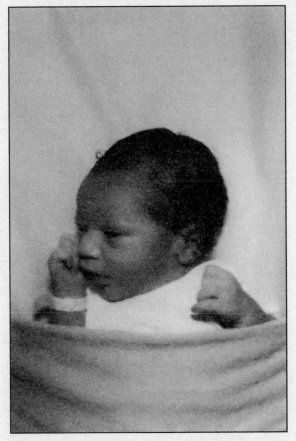

Me, just born and five minutes old.

name. He wanted his son to be smart, to be well educated, to understand that constantly learning and evolving is important. It was also important to him that his son should not just go with the status quo and be who everyone else wanted him to be but also to be who *he* needed to be—hence the name "Educated Rebel."

Baby me.

It's funny because, true to my father's belief, my name did end up affecting how I walked through life. Growing up, I was consistently told, "You're an educated rebel. You're a champion. You're the very best." And when you hear that every day, you start to believe it.

A lot of the traits I have, and why I'm the man I am today, come from hearing, over and over again, "You're educated" and "You're a rebel."

Inside the comfort of our home and family, I loved my name. I never questioned it. The first time I became aware that my name was different was when I was four or five. I had gone into a Jamaican restaurant with my father, who brought me everywhere. When we walked in, my father introduced me to the woman behind the counter, a friend of his. "This is my son, Karamo," he said.

Suddenly, I heard a voice behind us say with disgust, *"What's his name?"* It was a woman in line who was also Jamaican, and she was making a scene of it by loudly asking questions. I shrank into myself. It was the first time I had felt embarrassed by this gift my father had given me. I wanted so badly to turn and run out of that restaurant and wait in the car.

That didn't happen. My father held my hand and brought me closer to him. A charmer who also doesn't shy away from conflict, he immediately replied, in the sweetest of tones, "No, no, no, darling—this is a name you must know." Then he went into a speech. He explained the meaning of my name, and why as people of African descent we must honor the names birthed from our heritage. He expressed why uplifting one another—especially our children—is important, and why he appreciated her candor so he could have the opportunity to teach her this lesson.

At the end of his monologue, he basically had the restaurant applauding his words and my name. The woman apologized to me. This moment gave me so much pride to be my father's son and to have the name I do. After that, I would walk around saying to anyone who would listen, "My name is Karamo Karega," because my father made me feel that everyone should respect it and everyone should know it.

Dressing myself in khakis and a polo shirt.

But my troubles with my name were far from over—as I found out when it was time to register for kindergarten. I had been very excited. I already knew my entire alphabet and could count to five hundred. That's because my father would read and count with me almost every night—making sure I was educated and living up to my name.

Navigating the school system in Houston, Texas, where I grew up, took thoughtfulness. My father, per usual, was very strategic about this decision. He always made sure that, even during our many financial hardships, we always lived in the "best" school districts. Whenever we moved to a new apartment or house, my father would take out a map of the school zones to search for the housing line, in order to find a place in that area we could rent.

So thanks to my father's efforts to make sure we were always living on the side of a "good" school, I attended kindergarten at one of the best-funded schools with the best student/teacher ratio in the Houston district. But due to the way our educational system is set up in this country—which creates racial and economic borders that many people aren't able to cross—my father's efforts ensured that I only attended schools where the racial makeup was 99 percent Caucasian.

On the first day of kindergarten, I walked into school feeling excited and prepared. I also realized very quickly that there weren't any other African-American kids anywhere. This was a new experience for me. At that time, the Jamaican community in Houston was vibrant, and my parents quickly found that community, so I spent my time around other Jamaicans, Jamaican-Americans,

African-Americans, and Latinos—so much so that for a very short time in my life, I thought Jamaicans and Latinos were the whole population. I saw only a few white people.

I immediately knew that I was different from everyone else.

Now, I had always embraced my differences. As a child, I re-belled against the fashion choices available to kids my age. I used to wear khakis, a collared shirt, and a sweater-vest all the time. (And that was my choice: my parents didn't dress me, I dressed myself.) I wasn't into T-shirts and sneakers like everyone else my age, and that was okay with me. I didn't care that other students on that first day stared at me as I walked to my first class. I was still walking with the

Dressing myself in a sweater-vest and khakis again. It's a good look!

pride instilled in me from being in the cocoon of my very support-ive home environment.

However, my confidence quickly started to diminish within the first five minutes. I'll never forget what happened in that moment—not only because it shaped my identity for a very long time but also because what happened to me in that moment still happens to me today whenever I meet a new group of people.

I sat down at my desk, eager to learn. I had spent the last few years watching my sisters do school projects that seemed so fun to me. Now I was going to get the chance to do the same thing! The teacher came into the classroom, introduced herself, and welcomed us to kindergarten. She then took attendance. Sally (here), John (here), Christopher (here), Melissa (here).

But then it came time for her to say my name. "Kamo? Care-a-mo?" Each attempt was more painful. I don't remember her being malicious in any way—just confused by a name she had never seen before.

I said, "No, my name's Karamo Karega."

Then she blurted out, "What kind of a name is *that*?"

Immediately, the class was in an uproar as I shrank into my chair in embarrassment. This time, my father wasn't there to grab my hand and convince my teacher and my new classmates that my name was important. After that, I said maybe three words in that class, because I didn't want to bring any further attention to myself. To this day, the question I still get the most from strangers is, "What kind of a name is that?" But during that first day of kindergarten, I no longer wanted that name.

By the end of the first day, I had a plan of how to solve the problem of my name. If my father wasn't going to be able to protect me, I had to figure out how to protect myself. This is always how I've evaluated life. I'm a quick adapter. I figure out what my next move is and go after it without a second thought. It's my fiancé Ian's favorite quality about me. He often says, "You're so decisive—you always know what you want."

When I walked in the next day, I immediately went up to the teacher and told her, "Before you do attendance, my name isn't Karamo Karega . . . it's K.K." I knew in my heart that if I was truly going to enjoy school, I didn't need extra pressure. The teacher was probably relieved that she didn't have to butcher my name again, so she immediately agreed to my nickname and told me to take my seat.

A few minutes later, when she took attendance, she said, "K.K.?"

And I said, "Here!" There were no questions, and there was no laughter. And for the rest of my childhood, I was known as K.K.

Every day after that, if I was in a situation where somebody new was going to have to say my name out loud, I would immediately get to them before they would do it and say, "You can call me K.K."

My name shaped a lot of my actions. I studied harder so that no one could ever say that the kid with the funny name was also stupid. I had model behavior, because I never wanted anyone to say that the kid with the funny name was a problem child. I made sure I was heavily involved in school—I was in all the clubs in elementary school, and when I got to middle school and high school, I became the president of those clubs. I was an athlete. I did everything to make sure I fit in, because I didn't want to give anyone a reason to think I was different.

In the third grade, I remember going to the principal's office to speak with the principal—who refused to call me K.K. or to learn to say my name correctly—to ask if I could be the student who got to raise and take down the American flag each school day. At that point, he had given only white students the opportunity, and I wanted to change that. To be honest, even at that time, I could tell my principal was prejudiced against students who were different from him—whether that was due to their ethnicity, race, gender, or living with a disability.

I felt that he treated us differently in comparison to how he treated the Caucasian male students. It wasn't anything he said. The thing about prejudiced people is that you don't have to hear them say something to know they're prejudiced. He would walk down the hallways and high-five the white students and lower his hand when he got to me. Even at a young age, I knew why. It wasn't because of my grades—I got good grades. It wasn't that I was disruptive in class. There was no reason other than my differences.

I was determined to convince him that I could be the one in charge of the flag each day. I wanted him to realize that although I was different in his eyes, I deserved a chance to do it, because I was willing to work harder than everyone else to prove my worth to him. All I wanted was a yes—to know I had gotten the opportunity.

The only times I could ask him to please give me this chance were during my lunch break and after school. So on my lunch break, I scarfed down my lunch within three minutes, because I knew I had to ask my teacher if I could go to the principal's office. Then I ran to his office, quickly tucking in my shirt and wiping the sweat off my face to look as responsible and put together as I could.

The principal had a tiny office with a hall window that allowed a clear view of him sitting at his desk. He had a sweet receptionist, an African-American woman who in my young mind was seventy, but she was probably closer to forty. I anxiously asked her if I could see the principal, and she gave me a reassuring smile. "Of course, baby," she said. She called to tell him I was there—and through the window, I could see him pick up the phone and say something nonchalantly.

Then I watched as he sat at his desk and did not invite me in. Minutes passed. I nervously eyed the clock. More minutes passed. Finally the bell rang, and I reluctantly got up and went back to class.

This happened probably twenty more times.

Day after day, I never got a no, so I never felt defeated. He just ignored me, so I was going to come back. I was determined.

This is the child who sat outside the principal's office, petitioning him day after day. I believe I was eight in that photo, in the third grade.

I persisted, and I finally wore him down. When I got to see him, I begged him to give me a chance, which after several meetings he reluctantly did.

"You know you'll have to be here an hour early every day to do this job," he said, as if trying to discourage me. "And if it's raining, you'll still have to go outside and lower the flag."

I eagerly agreed. Once I finally had that yes, I'd get to school an hour early every morning in third, fourth, and fifth grades to proudly raise the American flag. To this day, I still know how to fold an American flag properly. It was one more way I combatted the perceived differences people conjured up in their minds when they heard or read the name Karamo Karega. That principal loved me by the end of elementary school and finally started calling me K.K.—a small victory.

Having a name that was considered exotic shaped my understanding of what it meant to be different in a country that doesn't always value people or ideas that aren't "normal." I kept the nickname K.K. until I got to high school, where I switched it from K.K.—which sounded too young—to Junior, and also Jayson Raine Brown. (Don't ask me where these names came from, because I'd be lying if I told you I knew.) Even though I had outgrown K.K., I wasn't ready to go by Karamo Karega yet. This became an awkward time for me, as friends would call my house asking for Junior or Jayson. My father would pick up the house phone and tell the person on the other line with certainty that they had the wrong number. Because I didn't want to cause any issues with him, I would dash to be the one to answer the phone anytime it would ring.

My three sisters—Marcella, a kind person who wants to make everyone's lives better and who is twelve years older than me; Nedra, a girly girl who was a track star and who is nine years older;

and Kamilah, a brilliant, athletic tomboy who is five years older—were all out of the house by then, so I had full domain over the phone. I just kept telling myself, *If I can get to the phone first, Daddy will never know that I go by Junior or Jayson at school, not Karamo*. But the secret didn't stay hidden for long. My father sat me down after school one day and asked me with genuine concern, "Why aren't you going by your given name?" And with the arrogance of a pubescent teen, I replied, "Why aren't you going by yours, *Henry*?" It was the first time I had ever called my father by his name.

In my household, it was extremely disrespectful for a child to call an adult by their given name. You called them "Mr." or "Mrs.," "Aunt" or "Uncle," but never by their first name. Especially your parents! I was terrified that I was about to get slapped for being disrespectful, but it didn't happen. My father just sighed and walked away. Ironically I didn't feel victorious in that moment—I didn't win that "fight." Instead, I had revealed a crack in my father's armor, and I also knew that I had exposed a crack in my own.

I went to school the next day and told my best friend Ray what had happened with my father and my name. He immediately said he would no longer call me Junior or Jayson, only Karamo, which eventually morphed into the nickname Ramo (Raw-mo). Somewhere in his young soul, he thought it was uncool that I was hiding who I was. Ray also made sure all our closest friends also only called me Karamo or Ramo. This started in my sophomore year and continued until I graduated. Though I had some of my friends calling me by my name at this point in my life, the pride that I once felt from being called Karamo Karega as a young child still wasn't fully back. The rest of the world knew me by another name, and I wanted to keep it that way. I felt more comfortable by not being different.

It wasn't until my freshman year of college, when I attended Florida Agricultural and Mechanical University in Tallahassee—a historically black university where I majored in business—that I officially started to go by Karamo. My dad pushed me to go to FAMU. He was watching me live two lives, have two names, and I think he hated it, though he never shared it with me. When he told me, "You have got to go to a black college," I didn't understand why. He had spent his entire life putting me in predominantly Caucasian schools and now was urging me to attend a historically black college where the student population was 99 percent African-American. Our relationship before I left for college had become extremely strained (which I'll get into later) but for some reason, I didn't fight his request to attend this university, though I had been accepted to several other schools. Something in my father's voice spoke to my soul and told me that this was where I needed to be.

The first day of my freshman year in college, I found myself surrounded by young, educated African-American students. I walked through campus, to the registrar's office for freshman orientation, and saw people wearing clothing that represented their African roots and sporting beautiful, natural hairstyles. At orientation, the freshman student greeter said, "Hello, my name is Kahremah." I was shocked, because I had never heard that name and was surprised at how close it was to my own. I replied hesitantly, "My name is Karamo." She gave me a smile and walked me to my seat.

Then a tall, beautiful African woman came onstage and stood in front of the anxious crowd of incoming freshmen to welcome us to our first day of college. She was a professor at the school and told us that she needed to see who was in attendance so she could distribute our dorm assignments. She pulled out her list and began calling names . . . Jonathan (here), Casey (here), Leah (here). I immediately panicked. I hadn't had time to tell anyone what my nickname was because I had gotten caught up in meeting that freshman greeter. I flashed back to that first day of kindergarten.

Not again, I thought. But then she got to my name. "Karamo?" she asked. I was so amazed she was saying my name correctly that I didn't answer immediately. "Is Karamo here?" After a few seconds of silence I finally came out of it.

"Here," I called.

She smiled. "What's the meaning of your name?" she asked.

"Educated," I told her shyly. "And my middle name is Karega, which means 'rebel.'"

"What a beautiful name!" she said, and then she continued on with the roll call. Not one student laughed or batted an eye. My name was normal there, and for the first time in many years, I was starting to find pride in my name again. Later that day I went to my dorm and introduced myself to my roommates as Karamo, and made sure I did the same in all my classes as well. It felt good to finally use the name my father had given me.

There were still times that people would mispronounce my name, but instead of shying away from the name I was given, or telling them to call me a nickname, I worked with them to teach them how to pronounce it and told them why it was an important name to me and my heritage. With each day, the pride of my name began growing stronger and stronger.

Yes, there were still days I wanted to be called K.K., or Junior, or Jayson Raine. I didn't always have the energy to teach someone why my name was special. But I also remembered what my father would say to me when I was a child—that I was an educated rebel, and it was my job to fight intelligently against the status quo in order to help others grow and see that our differences are gifts.

Today, I won't allow others to call me K.K. or any other name that isn't my own. It's not negotiable. I understand that some people may get it wrong . . . but I politely correct their pronunciation. Sometimes my old names still pop up. All my childhood friends, like my close friend from that time, Brian Bandy, only knew me as K.K. I hadn't heard from Brian in years and recently reconnected with him on social media. One of the first things in the message he sent to me was, "Hey, K.K.!"

I quickly replied, "It's no longer K.K.—it's Karamo."

It's interesting: my *Queer Eye* castmate Tan France's real name is Tanveer Safdar (France is his married surname). He doesn't go by Tanveer, for some of the same reasons that I went by K.K.—because we live in a culture where it can become increasingly exhausting for people to constantly have to explain their "different" name to others.

When we were preparing to shoot season 1, a curious crew member asked Tan why he didn't go by his birth name. Tan replied, "Because when you google 'Tanveer,' only terrorists come up. It's easier." Now, I love Tan—and I know he is not ashamed of his Muslim or Pakistani heritage. But Tan and I had a conversation directly after he shared his reasoning to the crew for wanting to be called Tan. This conversation happened in front of everyone and then continued when we were alone. I said, "Listen, you can be the one to change the public perception and image associated with your name. If our show is a success, when people google 'Tanveer,' they'll see your positive image. It's going to be someone who's doing good in the world. Think of all the little boys who are feeling the same way you feel and how you can inspire them to have pride in their name."

Tan is a very secure man who knows what he wants, and he quickly told me, "Nope, I prefer to go by Tan." I laughed and then shared with him that I had a similar issue when I was younger, when I would ask people to call me K.K. We bonded over our shared experience—and then I told Tan that he could call me K.K. if he wanted. He is the only one out of the Fab Five who calls me K.K. By allowing him to call me this nickname, it's my way of saying, "I understand our shared struggle. Hopefully through our conversations, one day you won't be Tan. One day, you'll want to be comfortable with the world calling you Tan-veer."

My struggle to accept my name resonates with so many people of color who have unique names, or who have immigrant parents. There are many people who feel different and just want to fit in—who don't want to have to explain who they are day in and day out. It was with my name that I realized, *I'm going to either have to fight to be equal, or I'm going to have to feel like I'm an outsider my entire life.*

My name is a gift given to me by my father. Right now, my relationship with him is broken and nonexistent. Afer years of conflict, my sexuality was the final nail in the coffin for him. There was never a specific phone call where we said we weren't talking again, or a fight that set us apart. It was one moment built on another that led us not to talk anymore. It was both of us making the decision that we did not agree with the other person's beliefs, so we weren't going to be in each other's lives.

This is probably the last photo I took of my father, right before our relationship went south. I loved his style. The glasses, the shirt—wasn't he smooth? I remember thinking, *I have to take a photo—my dad looks so cool.*

Despite this, I can acknowledge that my father tried to instill in me pride for who I am. Imagine struggling with your own demons but still working strategically to make sure your child has opportunities, giving him the tools to build bridges so people could learn about different cultures and experiences. Through my name, he gave me the ability to be free, to explore, and to be a leader. He engineered my life, starting with my name.

Any time I walk into a new space today, I'm conscious of the fact that people may assume I'm different from them because of my name or how I look. I now know, however, that self-love is the first key to combat that. I understand that I have to fall in love with my "differences." It's something I've mastered that others who feel different can master, too. I know I'm designed perfectly, from my name to everything else. It doesn't matter if others don't see it—I have to see it and believe it.

I tell myself positive messages about my name and heritage every day to outweigh others' negative opinions or ignorance, and I surround myself with people who do appreciate my uniqueness, which fuels me. I also check in with myself to evaluate how I react when other people have differences that I don't understand. Do I make faces, make comments, or ask questions that have an under-tone of superiority? The last thing I want to do is make others feel as if their differences are not special.

To this day, my father continues to battle with finding pride in his own given name. At least my conflict with my name has ended for me, and hopefully this will be the case for generations to come.

chapter two

The Pain of Colorism

When I was growing up, my family was what the kids nowadays call "woke." For their time, they were very aware of the realities of the world—especially when it came to race. In our house, we had very transparent conversations about the topic. Our family is a melting pot, to some degree. We have family members who are white, family members who are Cuban, and family members who are Jamaican.

We talked about race in a way that wasn't "them versus us." It was more "These are the things that are gonna go on, and you need to be aware of them." Our conversations were very matter-of-fact but still had an undertone of "Maybe things could change, if we all just try to see one another for more than our exteriors."

It was during these conversations as a child that I learned about colorism. Colorism is a prejudice or discrimination against individuals with a certain skin tone and is something that's been around forever in America and around the world.

During slavery in America, slave owners often granted more privileges to the lighter-skinned slaves, seeing them as smarter and more capable because of their white ancestry. Even after slavery ended, advantages were given to African-Americans whose appearances were closer to white, such as first consideration for certain schools and jobs. In the mythical post-racial America, it still remains true that the darker your skin tone, the less value the media, the justice system, and the educational system put on your life.

The first time I realized my skin tone was "bad" was when I was playing *Street Fighter*, a popular video game released in the late '80s. It was one of my favorites as a kid. After doing my homework and completing my chores, I would sit and play *Street Fighter* for hours.

Then *Street Fighter* came out with a new version of the game, where each of the characters had an evil twin who you could pick and fight against. While 99 percent of the characters were white or Asian, all their evil twins were darker in skin tone. It was hard for me to play the game, because the characters were supposed to be twins . . . yet the evil ones resembled black and Latino men.

One night after playing, I looked at myself in the mirror and wondered, *I'm dark, just like the twins. Does that mean I'm evil?* Many nights after that, I asked myself that question. I truly started to think, *There is no way I can be a good guy in life. I can't be the hero; I can only be the bad guy.* One day, I was playing *Street Fighter* with one of my white friends, and he wanted to be the evil twin. I couldn't accept that. I was black, so he had to be the good guy, not me. We ended up not playing the game, because he wouldn't let me be the bad guy. Of course, it was a warped way of thinking, but at that point, the subliminal messaging from my favorite game had really started to affect my mind.

To my family's credit, since we had many conversations about race, I was able to fight against the negative messaging. My mother, my father, and my sisters often talked about systemic racism, which is racism that's built in and infects every level of society, sometimes in very subtle or subliminal ways. I knew the word "racism" early on in life. Most kids don't truly understand what that word means until they're teenagers, but this was something we discussed constantly.

It was presented not in a way that was overbearing, but that was digestible at my young age. When we drove from an affluent neighborhood into a less affluent one, my parents would ask, "Do you see the difference?" Or when we watched TV and one character was depicted differently from another, they would ask, "Do you see the difference?" It was always spelled out for me in a way that didn't make me afraid but did make me aware. My family helped me realize that messages of colorism from mainstream or white-owned media were not who I was nor who I would ever be.

I always talk about the bubble of my house, where I felt very secure and very safe. I was aware of what was going on in the outside world, but it never fully affected me. I don't know if it was overcompensation on their part, but many of the white people I interacted with always told me how beautiful my skin tone was. I don't have early memories of white people telling me my skin was ugly.

I don't want to paint a picture that things were always rosy between me and other races—I did experience racism, and I watched my friends of color experience it, too. But I had been taught how to fight against that—with empathy and education. I would make an effort to channel any anger or hate I would feel and have it transform into love, and I would try to educate people of different races who held racist views rather than separate from them or stoop to their level. That's what my parents taught me to do. I didn't always succeed when I was younger, but I tried my hardest. But that's not what I want to focus on. There's another form of prejudice and colorism that is often not addressed or discussed.

Over the years, I realized that racism doesn't always come from the outside. People of color have also internalized these messages, and they negatively react to one another because of them. Now, my parents didn't prepare me for that. We never discussed how to combat the messages of prejudice when it's coming from members of your own culture.

The first person in my family who ever made me feel that my skin color was too dark was my granny. From the age of three, I went to her house on summer vacations. I loved my granny. This

Sybil Grant, my mother's mother, in 1960s New York.

was a woman who I respected deeply, who gave me so much life advice, who would say anything that came to her mind, who was a giver and a guide to many. On *Queer Eye*, I quote her constantly: "Never be afraid of growing slowly, only of standing still." She clearly had a big impact on me, but her influence wasn't all positive. Every summer when I visited her, she would tell me not to stay outside in the sun because she didn't want me to get darker—or, as she put it, "to darken up my family any more."

You know, when someone who you respect and love says to you, "Don't darken up my family any more," it sticks with you. As a kid, I understood from my parents that people outside my race might use my skin tone to make me feel bad, but this was my granny. This was a woman who raised me as if she were a second mother and taught me how to be empathetic, a good listener, and loving to everyone I came in contact with.

So what was I supposed to do or feel every time she said, "Don't darken up my family any more"? I didn't receive the tools on how to respond when someone who looks like me, who is in my family or of the same race, is saying things to make me feel bad about my skin tone. I would spend night after night in my granny's guest bedroom trying to process it.

To be honest, it hurt me more than most people can imagine. Beyond the fact that it was my beloved granny saying this to me, it also made me feel that what happened naturally to my skin when I was in the sun—what happens naturally to all of us when we're outside, being playful and having a good time—somehow made me bad. The emotions I felt from playing *Street Fighter* and thinking I was evil came rushing back.

I didn't have the courage to ask my granny why she would say this to me. Instead, I tried to please her by staying inside. I had a friend who lived across the street named Toby who used to be outside all the time, running up and down the street, having fun, doing everything I wanted to do. I would stand in my grandmother's beautiful bay window, watching him play, and think, *I can't go out there.* Toby was the same age as me, about the same height, but he had a much lighter complexion. As the summer days went on, his skin always turned a light caramel color. My granny would often say to him, "Toby, you're so sweet-looking." She never told me that, which I assumed was because of my darker skin tone.

Now, no one had told me that I couldn't go outside specifically. Still, I was so worried that if I did, Granny was going to say to me that I was darker, and that was bad. This wasn't something I discussed with my parents—I kept it inside. On my own, I stopped going outside until about four thirty or five, when the sun was going down. Unfortunately, I would have only about two hours to play with my friends, because by then, we would all have to start getting ready for dinner. So my summer days were spent staring out a window.

My grandmother is no longer with us, and I forgive her for those statements. She was a product of her environment. Her mother and father probably told her the same thing while she was growing up. They were living in a world where people didn't really talk about race. Their views had been birthed out of slavery and were still affecting the way they approached the world. My granny lived in an era where, in her mind, she had to have straighter hair and lighter skin and certain physical attributes so she could obtain opportunities.

I can't blame her for how she was conditioned, especially since I didn't have the language to help her grow. Still, her words stuck with me for many years.

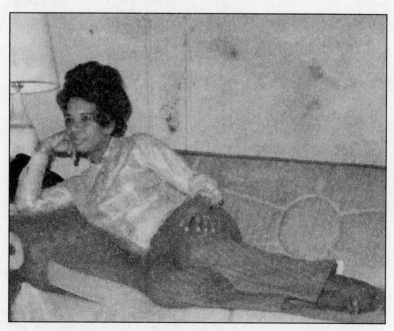

Granny Sybil, looking fly as hell in 1960s New York. She always dressed beautifully and did her hair beautifully.

———————

I had a similar experience in school. The first time I was ever called "darky" or "nigger" was by another African-American, when I was in the fourth grade. Now, we aren't talking about the 1940s or '50s or '60s here—this was the early 1990s. Again, I knew how to combat it if someone outside my race were to say something to me. But I never received the tools to say to someone who was in my race, "I don't appreciate you making me feel bad about the color of my skin."

Some of us kids were outside playing at recess. There was one other African-American child in my class. She was a very popular, outspoken, and beautiful young girl. Ironically, I just found her on social media, and she is nothing like I remember physically. I remember her skin being a lot lighter than mine, her standing much taller than me, and having a different hair texture than mine. In some old photos that she posted, I saw that had all been in my mind. She had beautiful darker skin then and she has beautiful darker skin now, but I think the language she used warped my memories into thinking she was "different" or "better" than me.

She was one of the first people to call me "darky" and "blackie." She would say that consistently to me throughout the years. Not because she was bullying me—instead, it was her way of joking with me. Like, if I would do something annoying, she would say, "Shut up, blackie. Shut up, darky." As an adult, I feel bad for that young girl, because I realize she used that language only because someone in her life must have said that to her in a "joking" manner, too. It was learned behavior that she was mimicking. As a child, all I knew was that those names made me feel confused and sad.

I knew that I didn't want to call her those names back. I did want to say something, but I never knew what. Growing up, I was not a kid who needed to trade insult for insult. That was never my style—I was very empathetic, which stopped me from disrespecting others.

I also felt like I couldn't complain about it. We were two black kids—what was I supposed to say? "She hurt my feelings, because she's black, and I'm black, and she's calling me 'blackie'"? It didn't make sense in my mind, so I did nothing. I felt like the only way that this insult would be acknowledged as something wrong by my principal or teachers was if she were white. If a white student had called me "darky," I would have gone to the principal immediately.

This went on throughout our entire time in elementary school together. After a while, it just became what she said and what I accepted.

Because of her comments, and those of my granny, my skin tone haunted me for a very long time and dictated a lot of my childhood. I would end up going home after school instead of playing outside so that I didn't get stuck in the sun too long. Or I would find a table in the shade during lunch, because our cafeteria was outdoors.

My parents used to tell me that if someone from another race said something to me about my color, I was to say, "This is how God made me. . . . I'm black and I'm beautiful." But if you look like me, you already know that God made me this way, because God made you this way, too. You know black is beautiful, or you should.

My school was maybe 95 percent white and 2 percent Asian, and the only person who called me by racist names was the other black kid in the school.

I would go home and be too embarrassed to bring it up to my mom, my father, or my sisters, because I figured they knew this was going on. When I was in middle school, I had another realization about the lighter skin/darker skin conversation. My sister had come home after school, upset that another African-American girl had said my sister thought she was "all that" because she was lighter. (Yes, the reverse happens, too, where people who are lighter-skinned are discriminated against because of a perceived privilege others think they have.)

I remember watching my parents jumping into action, saying, "This is what happens with women. They want to tell you that your hair's not right, that you're too light or too dark, but don't listen to it." They acknowledged her experience with colorism and let her know this was an issue that constantly happened to and against black women.

There I was, sitting at the table doing my math homework, riveted. For years, I had gone through this experience with this one girl, every day. And I had never had the courage to come home and talk about it. Now my ears were tuned in. As I listened, everything was about black women and colorism. Quietly, I said, "Well, that kind of happened to me, too." No one reacted. I said it again louder, and still no one reacted.

Because their thinking was, *You're a guy. You don't have these issues. Man up.* As I've gotten older, I've realized that their nonreaction is the same reaction I've seen in the media when it comes to black people talking about colorism—that gender plays a role as to who we sympathize with. Men's experiences dealing with colorism are too frequently left out of the conversation.

Instead, the public conversation about this issue centers around women: Black Girls Rock! Awards, Black Is Beautiful movement, hair product ads for women that say "Your natural hair is gorgeous." While I am happy that women of color have these resources, it hurts me that as a culture we don't also think about men's feelings when it comes to these issues.

You can find tons of memes about light-skinned guys versus

dark-skinned guys—such as how light-skinned guys act versus how dark-skinned guys act (which is all part of colorism). But I could not find any uplifting articles, songs, or programs—nothing—that spoke to my experience growing up as a man with darker skin or that gave me the tools to combat colorism.

As I got older, colorism, for me, took a different form. The language used by people in my own race toward me shifted to a tone much more hurtful than that which I was "supposed" to accept—and I began noticing a color fetishism happening.

At around twelve, I was in the football locker room before a game, and another young African-American guy walked in and, in front of everyone else in the room, said, "What's up, my nigga?" I immediately recoiled, hurt and disgusted. Somehow, I felt implicated even though he said it. I felt bad because of it, but I also sensed that if I didn't respond I wasn't "black" enough. *This is wrong*, I thought. *I shouldn't feel this way when someone greets me.*

It was a dagger into me every single time I heard that word. I've always hated the word "nigga." I recently wore a shirt on a red carpet that read NIGGER NIGGA NEITHER, with both "Nigger" and "Nigga" crossed out but legible. (Side note: I wore the shirt at a hip-hop television premiere event out of deliberate protest and rebellion because I knew that those words would be used casually there. It caused a lot of controversy because some African-Americans thought I was misguided while others supported the shirt.) Nevertheless, we are being conditioned by our own culture that it's okay to call one another this derogatory term, as long as nobody else calls us that.

How do I say to people, "Don't call me 'nigga,'" when every single hip-hop song I listen to says it is okay? When every single person in my circle of friends who is my age, and my race, is saying it? I was conflicted. I wanted to say, "That's not okay with me," but knew I would be ostracized or perceived as uncool if I did.

When it came to sex and skin tone, I would hear girls say about a guy, "Girl, you want him because he's darker. He'll probably be more aggressive and dangerous, and have a larger penis." Women would say this to me because that is what they had been taught. On the flip side, they didn't want to be in a relationship with me as much as they did the lighter-skinned guys.

I would hear comments like, "If we date someone lighter, our babies will be prettier, have better hair, have nicer eyes." This type of talk was, and is, damaging. The message I was getting from the world was that all I was good for was aggression and sex—while lighter-skinned black men could be emotional and create families. Everything was about "big black cock," and "the darker the berry, the sweeter the juice." This wasn't just from women but gay men, too. I realized that these negative messages were beliefs held closely not only by some in my race but by other races as well—

such as white, Asian, and Latino people, who I heard echo these sentiments.

It hurt. When I was a teenager, I made a conscious decision that I would play my "role." If that was what was going to get me positive attention, then I was going to be that guy—aggressive and sexual. This is what you expect of me, so why not live up to it? I became an oversexualized teen because of this messaging. It's no surprise that I had a child at sixteen (which I will get into later).

Colorism also affected my choice of the men I dated. For years, I had a specific type, which was the opposite of my skin tone. I hated talking about my preference for a long time, but now, because I no longer subscribe to this way of thinking, I'm open about it.

When you look at the men I dated, they all were six feet tall and light-skinned (or "high yella," as we call it in the African-American community). They had green eyes, or light brown eyes, and curly hair. If there was a guy who looked like that within five feet of me, I was dating him. He was my boyfriend.

Part of that preference came from media messages, as well as other black people, who were like, "Look how beautiful it is that the dark person and the light person got together." They applauded that. They loved that. Those couples were valued more. Think about Martin and Gina from the show *Martin*. Think about the Huxtables: Clair was lighter than Cliff. Think about George and Weezy from *The Jeffersons*: one was lighter; one was darker. Even today on shows like *Blackish*, you see the same pattern: Anthony Anderson is darker than his lighter doctor wife played by Tracee Ellis Ross. I love all these shows, but I want you to see how colorism is still in play subliminally within the African-American community. So it was always in my mind that in order to be a strong, beautiful couple, I needed to get someone who looked the opposite of me. My father is darker, and he married a lighter woman, too, so of course, I had to do the same.

At the time, part of me didn't realize that the self-hate behind colorism even affected those I chose to be with, but now I do. Getting pushed by my father to go to Florida A&M University was probably the best experience of my life, in so many different ways. It's where everything happened—I came into my own with my sexuality and I realized who I was. When I got to college and was on a campus full of only African-Americans, I got to a place where I matured into self-love. I began to realize the destructive ways black masculinity was tied up in colorism. On my college campus, there were people who were pro-black and loved their dark skin tones. There were people who were giving me the tools to fight back when someone in my own race perpetuated these color ideologies.

It was then that I began to proudly date dark-skinned men. (People will try to say on social media that colorism is still plaguing me, because I'm engaged to a white man. That's not true. There is a difference between seeking out a specific race or skin tone versus organically meeting someone and falling in love without pretense.)

In college, I remember being on the Set, which is what we called our main area on campus where everyone would hang out. There were rallies that didn't focus on how white people, or the mainstream media, treat us—they were talking about how we treat one another within our own race. A black campus was the first place I finally heard someone talk about colorism in the context of black women and men experiencing it within their own culture.

There was a path I would walk on to get to my dorm or class, and on the way, there were these pockets where students would congregate. Turn one way, and there would be a person on a soapbox talking about saving the environment, with a little crowd around him or her. Turn another way, and it was women's rights. One day on my way to class, I passed a man in a green army jacket and oversize black jeans talking to a crowd of a dozen students about dark skin and light skin. I stopped in my tracks and immediately joined the group. It was so empowering, and refreshing, to hear a man talking about this issue.

"The same way we don't disrespect our sisters for light skin or dark skin, we've got to remember our brothers," the man said, as everyone nodded. "When someone calls you a name, you have to educate them and let them know where that internalized racism was birthed from."

On my college campus, I started to realize that my being dark-skinned was cool. Walking through the president's hall, I would see men who were leaders of the university who were dark-skinned. Equally I saw the value in light-skinned men.

It was then that I learned comparison was killing us. It was robbing us of joy and connection, but our shared experiences made us strong and beautiful. Categorizing ourselves by our skin tone was self-hate, and we had to fight against it.

If someone on my campus said something negative to me about my race—like "Yo, black ass," there was always somebody else there to combat it. That gave me the courage to do it myself. It was in college that I gained the understanding that the only way to combat colorism, racism, and prejudice within my community is to acknowledge how it makes me feel and express, in a digestible way, why it is destructive to us all, and talk about how it is toxic to everyone's mental health.

When I became a father, I told my boys to go outside in the sun, and have the best time ever. I didn't want them to give up their childhood. I tell them all the time how beautiful their skin is. I have a different conversation than my parents had with me. If somebody says something about their skin tone, I have told them how to combat it. I tell them not to let it pass but to acknowledge it immediately. I tell them not to speak from emotion but from facts (because when it comes to race, people don't hear you anymore when you're speaking from emotion).

I tell them to be clear that they will not accept that language around them at all, because they're greater than those words. They should address the issue with someone in authority who can support them in correcting the other person's behavior. Finally, they should find me or someone else, so they can release those feelings, too. If you don't have an outlet to release it, it weighs on you, and starts to eat at you, and you may internalize it.

The conversation with my sons doesn't end there. It's important that we tell young boys how colorism is affecting their self-esteem and mental health. I want my sons to know that their skin tone has nothing to do with the goodness in their hearts and souls, and it does not define the success they will achieve in life.

Of course, I've also prepared them and made them fully aware of the systemic issues that they will be up against. They can fight through them, just like their father has. It's a different experience from mine, because I'm raising them in a world where I can identify how colorism is affecting them—not only outside the community but also from inside the community. That's how things have shifted in a generation.

That means if they're confronted with colorism within the black community, I have also given them steps to take. The first is to acknowledge that they're experiencing colorism from within their own race, the same as they would do if it was coming from the outside. It's okay to say, "You're discriminating against me because of my skin tone."

The next step is that they must express how the discrimination is making them feel. I think sometimes when you laugh it off, or you don't say anything, the person then thinks that the behavior is okay. That's just human nature—if you don't tell the person how those words are making you feel, then they might think it's all right to continue to say those words. If you don't have the confidence to speak up at that moment then you must find someone you trust who can be your voice—as you are finding the courage within yourself. Negative or ignorant behavior cannot be left unchecked.

Last, I teach my sons to challenge the person and ask them, "Why do you feel that that's okay? We are both of the same race." I warn them that sometimes people are not going to be open to listening. They'll say, "I've heard this many times . . . ," or "Aw, here we go. He wanna preach."

If that's the case, I tell them they can still walk away knowing that they planted a seed in that person's mind that is eventually going to get watered and grow. It will help them see that colorism is something that's affecting them. Today, I combat colorism by talking about it constantly. On *Queer Eye*, I bring it up a lot, because everything that's happening to us will happen to someone else. It's just the nature of the world. If you've given them the language of acknowledging it as discrimination, telling them how you feel, and challenging them, they'll have an opportunity to combat colorism in their own lives. I like to say, "The beautiful shades of the world are the colors of love that pour out from the light within us all."

chapter three

God Is Love

In my childhood years from early on, my mother, sisters, and I would go to Lakewood Church in Houston, Texas. Like clockwork, Pastor John Osteen preached every Wednesday night and Sunday morning. Lakewood Church is a nondenominational megachurch. It's global now, led by John's son Joel.

Faith was something that was very important to my parents when they were growing up in Jamaica. Christianity is a cornerstone of the island. My mother is a devout Christian, but my father is a Rastafarian, which caused conflict for them.

Religion has been ingrained into the minds of every person on the island of Jamaica since 1504, when Spanish settlers first introduced Catholicism to the native people. Religion then became even more important to the island as Christianity and the Church of England became the law of the land in 1655, when it was introduced by British colonizers. This history lesson never sat well with my father. As he began to learn more about his history, he began to research Rastafarianism.

People know Rastas because of Bob Marley, and they think they're just people who sit on a beach and smoke marijuana and talk about one love. There is a small element of truth in that, but it's not the full story. Rastafarianism originated in the 1930s among impoverished and socially disenfranchised Afro-Jamaican communities, as a reaction against British colonial culture and as an outlet for poor people to have a voice.

Rastafarianism is an interpretation of the Christian text, with a focus on self-empowerment and the belief that we have a higher destiny on earth. The conflict between my parents' religious views forced me to pick a side: Do I follow my mother and go to a Christian megachurch, or practice Rastafarianism with my father?

My mother ultimately won that battle and made sure that we were raised in a Christian household. As for me, religion wasn't something that I dreaded—it was something I had fun with. I was in a household where God didn't have a particular race or gender. My parents were very quick to interchange "he" and "she" when it came to God. That was key for me. Even though I would go to

Lakewood and hear them refer to God only as male, in my mind, when I was praying, I would switch back and forth between male and female.

My father would sometimes pray, "We ask God for her guidance . . ." So I'd think, *Oh, today God's a woman*. I don't know if he was even conscious of it, and then my mother picked up on it. Although Jesus is usually depicted as a white guy, I know that is someone's interpretation. I never took that as reality, because that wasn't how it was depicted in my household.

Going to Lakewood was profound, because although I had my Caribbean family members who I was close with and had tons of white friends from school, when I would go to Lakewood there would be people from every race. Lakewood had members who were Latinos, East Asians, South Asians, and Native Americans. Everyone was happy; everyone was loving one another.

Lakewood was a cultural playground to me. My friends who were Latino brought tamales for Bible study; my Cambodian friends brought traditional clothing items for us all to wear; others would bring in a toy from their culture that I hadn't known existed.

So I associated God and Jesus with enjoyment and the love that I had for my friends. Church was fun! I thought, *If this is what God and heaven are all about, sign me up!*

When I was maybe in the seventh grade, I developed a crush on one of my friends from church—let's call him Mateo. This is the earliest memory of my sexual preference coming into play, besides when I was six years old and thought boys were cute.

What I felt for Mateo at the time had nothing to do with sex or anatomy. It was pure in every way. I recall thinking, *Oh my gosh, I like being around him.* I didn't have a term for what it meant. It wasn't "gay" or "straight." I just remember thinking, *I feel giddy around you. This is fun. I want to spend more time with you.*

Mateo was a dark-skinned young Latino who was the same age as me. He had dark wavy hair—tight curls that almost went into an Afro but didn't. I don't know if he was Mexican or maybe Dominican, because at that age, I didn't have the language to ask. I just remember that he smelled so good.

I'd want to sit next to him every day in Bible study so that I could just stare at his tight, dark curls. Anytime we'd have to partner up to do anything, I needed to partner with Mateo.

I'm sure Mateo had no idea what was going on. He just thought I wanted to be his friend. I remember running down the hallways of Lakewood with Mateo, and I'd grab his hand. We'd be running and holding hands, in a very boyish, innocent way. In my mind, I was like, *Oh my gosh, I'm holding Mateo's hand.*

We would race. We would wrestle. We would eat together. In seventh grade, he was the reason I went to church. As I started to come into my own with my sexuality and comprehended in my mind that, to me, this was more than just a friendship I was having with Mateo, I started to realize something else. Even though Lakewood was (from my seventh-grade calculation) 95 percent full of love, there were people who could recognize that there was something a little bit . . . extra about my relationship with Mateo. And they didn't like it.

I would hear them make comments. *Why is he so close to Mateo? Look at the way he walks. Look at the way he's tucking in his shirt. Why does he scream like that when he's playing?*

Every time I would hear those comments, I would immediately correct my behavior. When you're way too aware, as I was, you start to monitor and change every one of your actions, because you're like, *Oops, I know I can't go that way because people are judging me, so I'm going to go this way instead.* It hurt, being judged by adults for things I couldn't control. I would find moments alone in the back corner of the church, where I would just put my back against the wall and take deep breaths in order to keep myself from crying.

I started to hear those comments more frequently as my friendship with Mateo grew. I don't think Mateo heard them, because he never reacted to them, or maybe he did but just didn't care. I wanted to talk about how I was feeling, but didn't know how. Even though I didn't have the words to describe who I was, I knew something was going on. I knew I never looked at the girls in my Bible study or in my classroom at school the same way I looked at Mateo.

The homophobia I remember as a child never came from my peers: it only came from adults. Being the kid who was fully aware,

I could change things up pretty quickly. Kids weren't able to catch on to my being "gay," because again, I would quickly correct my behavior.

Even though I heard those comments from some of the churchgoers at Lakewood, it didn't make me feel bad about church. I was able to understand that these people were immature adults making derogatory comments about a child. I knew that what they were saying under their breath was wrong, but I didn't speak up—my parents always taught me that as a child, you shouldn't speak to adults a certain way.

So I ignored them. I still loved going to church. I'd think, *This is still a great place. I'm going to get to see Mateo; I'm going to run around; I'm going to get to read the Bible, and eat, it's going to be great . . . no matter what some of the adults say.*

Even to this day, like on the *Queer Eye* episode where Bobby and I talked about the impact religion had on us, I say that I love the church. I have a great relationship with God. Bobby and I are different in the sense that he equates people's ignorance with church. I've separated it and said, "Your individual ignorance has nothing to do with my experience with God. This is not of the church. This is you."

My feelings about the church did change for a while, though, when a new Bible study teacher came in on a random Wednesday night. She was a blond woman with a thick Southern accent whose name I can't remember. Usually our lessons were very much about how to give back, or how to make friends through the love of Christ—basic Bible concepts that children could understand.

This woman came in with a mission that altered my experience at church. I was sitting next to Mateo's gorgeous self, enjoying church like always. Suddenly, this woman started talking about how young people will be pressured to have "impure thoughts," and how we have to fight against them. I was in the seventh grade, and it was not appropriate for her to be talking about that, especially without our parents being around. As a father, I would have said, "If you're going to have that conversation, let me know so I can be around and support my kids and answer any questions that they may have." This was, to my knowledge, a group of kids who never, ever had "impure thoughts." I know that, personally, I was not even thinking about sex. Just to sit next to Mateo was all I wanted.

I think about the other kids in there who had crushes. We weren't "fast kids," and we were in a safe church environment. We were happy just to look at someone—no sex or kissing needed. This woman went on and on, telling us that if we kiss or touch anyone, we would go to hell. Then she started preaching about homosexuality. She said that if you are a boy and you like another boy, you are definitely going to go to hell, because that is wrong in the eyes of God.

I will remember that moment forever. Immediately, I scooted my chair away from Mateo. I thought to myself, *I don't think I want to have sex with him! But I do want to be close to him. Is this impure? What am I doing?* I moved quickly, out of fear of going to hell.

That evening, Mateo and I were walking to go get our parents, who were in the big church. He said to me, "Hey, let's race!" Like we had always done, which always led to us innocently holding hands.

"Nope," I said. "I can't be around you anymore." I had spent two years cultivating an amazing friendship with Mateo prior to my crush, and in one fell swoop, I shut it off. Because this woman came in, and in my mind, she clocked me.

"Clocked" is a gay term that means "I see that you're gay, or part of the community, even if you haven't expressed it." As an adult now, I see that she had her own baggage that she was trying to drop on us. Something happened in her own life. She was probably going through issues with her own sexuality. Maybe she'd just kissed a girl and liked it. She was probably a literal Katy Perry song and was coming in there to vent to kids because it was on her mind. Or she may have been struggling to accept the sexuality of someone who was close to her. Who knows what she was going through? But it wasn't her job to discuss sexual orientations or identities with kids and scare them into believing that anything they did was going to send them straight to hell—whether straight or gay.

After hearing this "lesson," the way that I approached my sexuality changed. I could adjust to comments about how I walked or that my bow tie was tied a little too tight. Those were physical things I could change, but my sexuality was bigger. After that, I remember very distinctly going home and realizing that my father and his friends and relatives talked about homosexuality in the same derogatory way.

It was the kind of toxic male behavior that you see everywhere—wherever a group of men congregate at school, at a job, in their family. It's ignorant language that they use to appear tougher or more "manly." In the case of my father and his friends, it would quickly go from joking to a torrent of blatant homophobia. It would be as simple as my uncle doing something that the others would perceive as "acting gay." If one of my father's friends walked across the room in a certain way, for example, one of them would say, "Stop acting like a faggot." If someone threw a beer in a way that they perceived as having the characteristics of a gay man, it was "You throw like a faggot." Or they would bring up certain Bible verses in their discussions, like the one about how "Thou shalt not lie with mankind, as with womankind."

I had never really paid attention to their talk, but this woman had opened my consciousness up to this hate. Suddenly, I couldn't turn a corner, couldn't turn on the TV or listen to music, without hearing about it.

I was in so much conflict. Church was a place that had been safe for the past six years of my life. It was fun. Suddenly, I was being told that it was not safe.

It's important to note that I didn't have the words to define how I was feeling about Mateo. This is why I always tell people: "Don't oversexualize children, because they often don't have the language that adults assume they have." We put these adult concepts on children when it comes to sex and sexuality, and we don't realize that often they aren't even thinking about it. The reason kids become oversexualized, or they become depressed, is because we start putting these words in their heads when they're too young. What we should be doing is having healthy conversations with them that help them better understand their feelings, and encouraging them to realize that their feelings are natural.

My "relationship" with Mateo was innocent. Now, because I was being told that I must want to lay with another man, I started thinking about it all the time. I thought, *Oh, I guess I must want to have sex with Mateo. I guess I must want to kiss Mateo.* Then my next thought was that this teacher says I'm going to hell because of that. Mateo was the catalyst for the fire and brimstone that was going to come to me, because I liked looking at his dark curly hair. So I completely shut down our relationship. If he approached, I would push him away. After a while, he stopped trying.

It was a very sad time for me, because it was like I had lost my best friend. I don't just mean Mateo—I mean the church. I loved everything about the church, and now my best friend was gone. The love and the fun weren't mine anymore, because I was different. And I knew I was different.

My eighth grade yearbook. I had just stopped going to church and remember spending Sundays looking at my yearbook over and over because I no longer carried a Bible.

Soon after that, I stopped going to church on Wednesday nights. Then, maybe a year later, when I was in eighth grade, I quit going on Sundays, too. The reason I was able to do that was because my Rastafarian father didn't believe you had to go to church to have a relationship with God. When I said to my father, "I don't want to go to church," there was no pushback. He overruled my mother and said, "Great, you take your daughters to church, and my son will stay home with me."

Of course my mother protested, but my father said, "No, he doesn't want to go. He still says he loves the Lord. He's here with me. We'll pray and read together." Well, I knew how to get out of that. My mother and sisters would go to church, and my father would take out his Bible and read it. He is a very spiritual man, and I knew that he was more of a silent reader. It was very easy for me, after five minutes, to tell him I needed to get up and go to the restroom.

Then I would never go back. He was so engrossed in his own religious experience that he would forget I had left. I started spending my Sundays on the couch, watching cartoons and *Saved by the Bell* reruns. I didn't have to go to church anymore because Dad stopped it, and my soul was saved from burning in hell because I wasn't near Mateo anymore.

As I started going through eighth grade, I hated that I stopped praying to God. I hated that I stopped being a part of something that was bigger than me. It was on my mind constantly. I wanted to go, but I didn't want to be clocked again.

On Easter Sunday in my eighth-grade year, my mother forced me to go to church. On this Sunday, John Osteen kept saying, "God is love." Each time he spoke those words, it hit me like a bolt of lightning. That simple, three-word statement was big for me. In that moment, I realized that I knew how to get back my best friend, the church. If I stopped thinking about sex with boys and instead thought about a boy as someone I wanted to love, then I would be okay with God.

There you go, Karamo. Problem solved. God is love, so if you love men instead of sexualizing them, then you and Mateo can be together! It works because God is love! If I'm going to be of love, and of God, then my looking at Mateo in a loving way works.

That shift right there was major for me. It then became the benchmark for every conversation I had from there on out, for everyone who would try to challenge my sexuality.

It also became the benchmark for why I have only been in long-term relationships. I'm a serial monogamist. I've been in only long-term relationships since I was fifteen, going from one to another. Some people say I'm codependent, because I've never been single.

I had my first (and only) girlfriend when I was a teenager (which you'll read about later). I broke up with her and had my first boyfriend. I stayed with him for two and a half years. In college, I stayed with my boyfriend for two years. After I left him, I was with another boyfriend for two and a half years, then another for four years. I left him to get into a relationship with my kids—I didn't date anybody, because I had to focus on them. Then I met Ian, the man I am spending the rest of my life with.

There you have my romantic history. I didn't have any dates in between. Don't get me wrong—I'm no angel. I've cheated on boyfriends. Even the few times I cheated I would always tell myself, *This happened because I was lustful. That was wrong. My relationships are supposed to be about love.* It always went back to that statement, which has gotten me back on track.

God is love. I thought, *If I do this in love, then I'm okay.* So I fully returned back to the church.

I came out at fifteen, although I don't use the term "coming out." I say "letting people in." I think the term "coming out" gives other people the power to accept or deny people who identify as LGBTQ+ and takes the power away from those who should really own their power. Like my granny would say, "If they don't want to come in my house, I'll close the door and be happy in my own home." That was clear with me, because if you don't want to come into my life, that's fine. The power of me loving and accepting myself is not determined by someone else's opinion of me.

I also realized that the term "coming out" puts unnecessary pressure on members of the LGBTQ+ community. We don't need to let everyone in to every part of our lives. It doesn't mean that we're ashamed of who we are. It's called "boundaries." If we're not close friends, you don't need to know what I'm doing at home.

We put so much pressure on LGBTQ+ people to come out to everyone. It's like, "Okay, I'm at Thanksgiving dinner, and there's this random person who came with my cousin who I don't even know, but I now have to let them into my life. I don't know you! I don't have to 'come out' to you."

Being selective about with whom I share I am gay doesn't make me ashamed. I have clear boundaries on respecting myself and respecting my life. People always ask me if I have a coming-out story.

I don't. I knew at fifteen; I told a few friends who I trusted, then I told some more people, and boom, I was "out." Great—y'all know. The end.

I think the confidence that I had in myself and the fact that I found a "tribe" that supported me was critical in feeling empowered as a young gay man. I was never bullied, even though I played team sports like football and ran track. Normally, people assume those spaces encourage a culture of homophobia, but that's not always true. It certainly wasn't true for me.

I always presented myself to others, especially my male straight friends, in a way that let them know I did not want them in a sexual way. I would ask them, "Are you attracted to every woman you see? Then why would you assume I am attracted to every man I see? That's your ego and a bit of homophobia making you assume that." I told them very clearly that the men I dated were men I thought I could fall in love with. I think this gave many of my young peers a sense of ease that I wasn't "attracted" to them, but I didn't say that to make them feel more comfortable. I said it because that was my truth. That was how I was right with God.

Now that I was back in church, I began fully letting people close to me into my life. I also realized that the rebellious side of me would not let someone say something negative about the LGBTQ+ community in my presence while at church.

That quickly became my fight and my mission. I'd be sixteen, seventeen, eighteen, going through church, and if someone said, "You know, God says man shall never lay with man," or brought up Sodom and Gomorrah, I was there to combat them. I summoned the courage by going back to little Karamo in the seventh grade, who almost lost his best friend, the church.

I would feel compelled, even if I didn't know the person. At this point I was well researched in the Bible and used that knowledge to fight against those who spewed hate. I would assert that what they said was wrong, let them know how this made others feel, and then drop some knowledge on them.

Divorcing verses from their context is the biggest mistake people who read the Bible can make. You can't twist verses into something they were never intended to mean. People would always try to divorce scripture from context with me. It's very easy, when you have a book, to pick one line and say, "Look what this sentence says." But it's like, "Girl, read the rest of the paragraph."

If you're going to interpret the Scripture, then you must do it honestly and in context. I know my Bible verses. Every scripture I look for, I look for love and how love plays into it. When you start thinking about love, you realize there is no judgment. I came to the realization that there is no actual indication—cultural, historical, religious, or linguistic—that lesbians and gays are wrong. Ever.

And this is in every version of the Bible, from King James to whatever else you've got. Never. None. I have done the research, because if I'm going to talk about this, I want to be well informed.

In 1 Corinthians 6:9–10, it says, "Know ye not that the unrighteous shall not inherit the kingdom of God? Be not deceived: Neither fornicators, nor idolaters, nor adulterers, nor soft, nor abusers of themselves with mankind, nor thieves nor covetous, nor drunkards, nor revilers, nor extortioners, shall inherit the kingdom of God."

This is actually about sex between masters and slaves, sex between adult men and adolescent boys, and prostitution. In all those cases, men used sex to express power, dominance, and lustfulness, not self-giving love and mutuality. Committed same-sex unions between social equals represent very different values than the types of same-sex behavior Paul would have intended in 1 Corinthians 6.

Or Romans 1:26–27: "For this cause God gave them up unto vile affections: for even their women did change the natural use into that which is against nature. And likewise also the men, leaving the natural use of the woman, burned in their lust toward another; men with men working that which is unseemly, and receiving in themselves that recompence of their error which was meet." In the full context of Romans 1 this had nothing to do with prohibiting loving relationships but was a warning against idolatry, pagan cult images, and pagan rituals.

Or how about the cliché that Christians often use with regards to homosexuality: "Hate the sin and not the sinner." Nowhere in the Bible does it say that. It's actually a quote from Gandhi!

A few years ago, I was on a VH1 special about hip-hop and the LGBTQ+ community, and I got into it with a pastor who believed that homosexuality is a sin. I was like, "There is no way you are going on national TV and telling people that how they love is wrong. You think I'm going to be silent while your words trigger and traumatize the people on the panel or watching at home? Not on my watch."

Did the pastor change his mind? Nope. The only positive thing that came out of that conversation is that I got hundreds upon hundreds of letters from people saying, "Thank you for speaking on our behalf. It was like me talking to my pastor." I think most gay men of color had never seen someone who was like them stand up to a pastor. In African-American culture, you're taught that there are certain people you just have to defer to—your pastor, your parents—which doesn't allow for respectful conversation between people with opposing views. You are taught that by challenging a pastor, you are somehow challenging God, which is not true. This way of thinking breeds a culture of unhealthy power dynamics, where it's "my way or the highway."

By the way, that homophobic pastor ended up getting divorced— his ex-wife is on *The Real Housewives of Potomac*, and she put out their business! She talked about how he cheated and they got divorced, and the hardships he has had since then. I'm not gloating about his misfortune, but a good Bible verse to bring up here is "He that is without sin among you, let him first cast a stone at her." God don't like ugly, so check your ugly behavior!

I worked through my trauma in seventh and eighth grade. It took me a year and a half. Now I challenge people all the time—people who say they're Christian, or religious, or spiritual. I say, "Just show me the facts. If you show me a fact that disputes what I'm saying to you, then great. But you can't do it. You're showing me a verse, and divorcing it from context, and I will not allow that."

The verse that trumps them all is 1 John 4:7–8, which reads, "Beloved, let us love one another, for love is of God; and every one that loveth is born of God, and knoweth God. He that loveth not knoweth not God, for God is love."

Still to this day, I get into conversations about supporting religion as a gay man. Even on *Queer Eye*, this is an issue I discuss with Bobby—my castmate and the designer on the show. He and I are so close. I love him with all my heart. He also grew up in a religious community, in Missouri, and felt that his church turned its back on him when everyone found out he was gay. It hurts me to my core that he has lost a relationship with something bigger than him. In the season 2 premiere with Mama Tammye, which partially takes place in a church, he refused to even step inside of it. He gets upset, he cries about it—and the reason he gets upset is that the trauma is still there.

It's because that goes deep. When something tells you that you're not right, it affects your overall mental health. It's saying that the universe does not like you.

My son Jason identifies as an atheist. It's because his grandmother on his mother's side is very religious, and she uses religion—from his point of view—to be hateful. She has said hateful things about me as a gay man in front of him. This is his way of combatting against that hate. It's his way of saying, "No, my father's a good man, he takes care of me, takes care of my brother, and is full of love and positivity. If you're spreading hate, I'm not going to be about it."

Would I like my son to come back to the church? Of course I would, because I want him to know God's love. I used to take him to church all the time, because I wanted him to see me, as a gay man, in that atmosphere feeling comfortable and okay, and able to fight against any conflict that someone has with my sexuality.

He's seen me do it, but he's a different soul than me. I'm a fighter, and I've run toward conflict my entire life. Jason, on the other hand, doesn't want to fight against everything. He just wants to be happy and for others to be happy. He's a lover and a nurturer.

He's like, "If I have to do what Dad does and fight constantly in this space, I don't want to do it. If I can't see this thing called 'God,' how do I even know God exists?"

We have transparent conversations about it. Since he's on his journey to figure out his spirituality, I don't pressure him. If God is love, I have to love Jason as an atheist. I can't tell him he's wrong.

That one simple statement I heard from John Osteen when I was in the eighth grade still sticks with me to this day. That's why when people react negatively to my telling them that my son Jason is as an atheist, I reply, "I'm not raising Jason as an atheist. I'm loving Jason as an atheist."

These days, I attend a traditional black church. It's a great church, and the pastor preaches love. Yes, there are members of the congregation who have conflicting feelings about homosexuality and religion. But guess who is in the space to help them clarify their feelings? Karamo.

I love going to church and communing with people who are different from me. I love meeting, and fellowshipping. I love when they say, "Turn to your neighbor and tell them that they're special." I love at the end of the sermon when they say, "Hug somebody you don't know." These are things that I love. I don't want to give them up. Any person who is of LGBTQ+ identity who feels they have to give it up but don't want to—I just try to let them know that hatred is not God. That is someone's ignorance.

To me, there's always a place for church. The same way you go to a club and have fun and meet new people and learn new things—that's how we can think of church. If you're not having fun, you need to go to another church. You should walk out of church smiling, with some pep in your step.

The reason that churchgoing numbers are declining is that people are tired of hate. They don't want to go into a place where they're going to be told that someone they love is wrong, or that something they do is wrong.

They want to come to a place where they feel embraced and not judged. Where they feel loved. If more churches would go back to that core idea that God is love, then more people would stay. I walked out in seventh grade, but I'm grateful I came back. I faced that conflict and won with the love of God on my side.

chapter four

Overcoming the Legacy of Abuse

When I was growing up, physical and emotional abuse were a part of my household, and a part of my family's history. My father has never shared with us how the household he grew up in shaped him, but from what I gathered, abuse was prevalent.

In my home, my mother was abused by my father repeatedly. There are many stories I want to share, but my mother and sisters have not dealt with their emotions and the trauma that lingers within them when it comes to the physical and emotional abuse doled out by my father.

Out of respect for them, I will talk about my own experience. My connection to the abuse my father dealt out is a very odd one, but it affected me nonetheless. Growing up, my father wrestled with many demons. In my opinion, he was depressed, angry, dealing with addiction, and unsure about where his life was going. My father was also very . . . I don't like using the word "strict," because it has a negative connotation, so let's say "disciplined." He was very clear on the rules of the house, but those rules weren't extreme. There were no "Daddy Dearest" moments. It wasn't as if we had to get up at 5:00 a.m. and do an extreme amount of housework.

His rules were just very clear—things like doing all your schoolwork on time, keeping your room tidy, being respectful of your siblings and to adults. When those things weren't done, the punishment was usually some type of spanking—for one of my sisters, that is, but never me.

From the age of three or four, I understood very clearly the confines of my father's rules, and since I usually respected them, I didn't get punished often. Even the few times I was on his radar for a misstep, he would always sit me down and have a conversation with me so that I could learn the difference between right and wrong. These conversations were really big for me as a boy. Having my father talk to me like a young adult taught me the importance of having clear and constructive conversations with others about negative behaviors.

However, my sister didn't get the same courtesy of a conversation that I did—she just got spanked. Yes, my sister probably did push the boundaries more than I did, but in my opinion, nothing she did ever warranted the spankings she got. When I say "spankings," I don't mean beatings with a closed fist. My father never punched her, never pushed her to the ground. It was what was culturally acceptable at the time in many communities in the United States—an open-hand slap on her behind, and later in life the use of a belt. Now, this is something that I don't agree with. Because it is not "just spanking." Many of us have been conditioned as a culture that spanking is not abuse, but we should stop qualifying this in our minds. Let me be clear on my opinion: when someone puts their hands on a smaller human being, it's abuse.

The spankings I witnessed my sister getting were one of the reasons I eventually decided, at the age of twenty-two, that I wanted to work in social services. Every article I have ever studied on child welfare indicates that corporal punishment is an ineffective, unnecessary, and harmful form of discipline for parents to use with children. Despite that knowledge, some parents today still believe that in order to raise a compliant and well-behaved child, corporal punishment—including spanking, hitting, and slapping—is necessary. But it's not, and when I was young, it scared me.

When I was a child, there was nothing I could do about my sister's spankings. I just had to internalize it and secretly vow to protect her when I got older. As the spankings were happening to her, my father was also consistently abusing my mother.

My father's abuse of my mother was always hidden from me—something that, to this day, I have never witnessed with my own eyes. I was always shielded from my father's wrath, always protected from it.

My mother and father, about ten years after their divorce.

The first time I realized the abuse was happening was one night when I was five or six. It was around one o'clock in the morning, and my father had just come home. He drank a lot, beers mostly, and smoked a lot of marijuana. I heard some kind of loud commotion in the house that scared me, and I was instantly awake.

I slowly got out of my bed and walked to my door, which led directly into the upstairs hallway that overlooked the downstairs.

The minute I walked out into the hall and looked down at the scene below, it was as if my mother, my father, and my sisters all froze in time. All commotion ceased as they stared up at me in alarm. Then everybody started moving at once. One sister grabbed my arm; another put her hand on my back. Without any discussion, they calmly brought me into the bedroom and told me to go back to bed. "Everything's going to be okay," they told me as they shut the door, and darkness filled the room again.

I couldn't go back to sleep, so I got up and pressed my ear against my bedroom door to listen—as if on cue, the noise and the abuse and the screaming started happening all over again.

The next day, my mother called me to the table to eat breakfast before I had to catch the bus for school. As she walked from the fridge to the stove to me, I caught glimpses of bruises on her body that peeked through her robe. I don't recall ever seeing any bruises on her face, which I later learned was something my father did deliberately. By hitting other parts of her body, the abuse became a secret that she had to keep. It also put the shame of being abused on her. It made her feel as if she was being complicit by hiding the abuse, too. The abuse became our family secret—one that caused a profound sense of guilt for my mother as a survivor of it.

On those days when I caught glimpses of my mother's bruises,

I'd spend a lot of time trying to figure out what had happened to her. I'd try to make connections: *This has to be the result of last night.* No one talked about it, and I was so young that I didn't have the words to express my anxiety about what was going on. When I got older, maybe around ten or eleven, I began to question the older members of my family—aunts, uncles, and close friends of the family who we called "aunts" and "uncles." I'd ask them, "Is Daddy hitting Mommy?" They were still hesitant to tell me the truth, not wanting to say yes or no.

Though my father was abusive, he could also be a total sweetheart. He would give my mother flowers, or leave some romantic handwritten note on the bed for her. It was never directly after the abuse—never that type of patterned behavior, like, "I did something, so now I'm being nice to make up for it." He was just genuinely sweet to her, which confused the situation even more.

Every so often, he would wake the entire family up at three in the morning, and we'd all get in the car and go to this restaurant called Champs. It had this toy train that ran across the top of it, and they served all-you-can-eat pancakes through the night. To a young boy, it was the best time ever: Daddy's waking us up to take us to the place with the toy trains and the pancakes with blueberry and strawberry syrup! Back then, it was amazing; it was family time. Now though, as an adult, I understand that he did this only because he would come home drunk and this would be his way of saying "I'm sorry" to his family.

Once I realized my father's abuse was happening, I felt embarrassed and upset that my mother was staying with him and making excuses for him—that she still loved a man who abused her. For a while, I wondered, *Well, maybe, did Mommy do something that made him mad? Was she cheating on him?* But the answer was always no—and even if it were yes, that would still be no justification for my father's behavior.

As I became a teenager, I found myself thinking very often about the abuse my mother suffered at my father's hands and about seeing the spankings that my sister got. By this point, my parents were divorced, my sisters were in college, and I was living alone with my father. Each time I thought about what he did to the women in my family, rage would boil inside of me, which I would try to channel into being protective of the other women in my life. It got to the point where in middle and high school, I would get involved if there was ever a friend or a stranger who raised their voices at or talked negatively to a woman.

I became this protector of women I perceived were experiencing abuse. I couldn't turn my back and allow it to happen as I did when I was a kid. I was older, and I was going to say something. I wasn't able to protect the women in my family, but I would protect these other women.

This "savior" behavior continued in college. In my dorm, there was a common area with a kitchen, which you had to pass through to get to the bedrooms. One time when I was walking through there, I heard screaming from one of my roommates. He was in a verbally abusive argument with his girlfriend, and I knew he had a predisposition for violent behavior. Without thinking, I literally jumped in between them, chest puffed up and arms out, like that famous Michael Jordan "wings" poster. "You need to stop talking to her that way," I said. "Stop screaming at her."

His girlfriend started hitting me and told me to get out of the way, so I did. (But the next day, I saw a bruise on her face. Even though I had tried to help, I was upset to see that the abuse had still happened.)

There have been only two times in my life and career that I've ever gotten out of line with a woman—not being physically abusive but saying something that I regretted later because it resembled the abusive language I heard my father use while I was growing up. When I was twenty-two and on MTV's *The Real World: Philadelphia*, I started calling my roommate Shavonda a slut for sleeping with one of our male castmates. And on the reality show *The Next :15*, which I was also on, I called my castmate Tiffany "New York" Pollard the b-word. Both times I felt horrible afterward, and so embarrassed. I felt as if I had failed not only my younger self but my mother and sisters as well. I had raised my voice and called these women derogatory names.

Those moments when I failed didn't stop my rescue fantasies. What I realized very quickly, however, is that when you start engaging in other people's relationships, especially when there's abuse involved, the women being abused aren't always ready to accept help. Many even try to protect their abuser.

This is something I experienced with my mom—she protected my father throughout their relationship. To this day, my sisters still have a good relationship with my father. Still, none of this has ever discouraged me from trying to help other women.

Today, I understand that domestic violence is extremely complex, and that there's only so much you can do as an outsider to stop it from happening. It's never an easy task for people to leave an abusive relationship. I now get that my job wasn't to jump in the middle of these disputes but instead to let these women know I was concerned and would always be there when they needed me. My job was to listen and support their decisions, give them resources to use when they were ready, and encourage them to take small steps toward a different life. When I was younger, I thought that you protected women from being abused by being violent toward the men who were abusing them.

Even though I knew it was wrong for women to be hit, I was taught the message that if it's a man you're arguing with and it escalates to violence, that's normal, because men sometimes need to fight it out. My father never spanked me. Instead, he tried to help me understand boundaries through care and conversations. As I got older, though, I picked up on the power dynamic in our family.

My father was able to abuse my mother and spank my sister and get away with it, without suffering any consequences. He was never scolded by any family members, never arrested.

Even when you're protected from it, the trauma of abuse has a way of finding you. If you had told me when I was a kid that I would one day repeat my father's pattern and be physically abusive to my own boyfriends, I wouldn't have believed you. Yet that became my truth.

Although I would defend girls from their abusive boyfriends in high school and college, I'd also always be the first one who would want to physically fight the guy in order to protect them. It shocks me now how often I was putting myself in a position to fight to protect someone else. Ironically, I was trying to stop violence with violence, which I see now as an adult is the wrong way to do it.

Even though I learned that it is bad to hit women, men were still fair game. This wasn't just taught in my house—it was something that was culturally acceptable, too. If a young boy hit a girl on the playground, it was a big issue. If two boys engaged in any aggressive or violent behavior, it was described as "boys being boys." I heard that my entire life, and it became the norm for me.

From the ages of twenty to twenty-four, I was completely emotionally and physically abusive to the men I dated. My trigger could be something as simple as having a bad day. I would come home and just start verbally berating the person I was with. I justified it by thinking, *I'm down, so I'm going to tear you down, too, right now.*

The minute my partner talked back and the argument escalated, I hit him. My best friend Ray, who is straight and is my own little spiritual guru, witnessed a lot of this. He would always say, "Funny how you get mad at me if I raise my voice at a girl, yet you like to knock out every boyfriend you have."

Instead of taking the time to think, *Wow, I need to reflect on this*, my reaction was to make a joke. I'd say, "Yeah, because he deserved it," or "We are two men and the same size, so it's fair." It was a sick perspective, but one that many people share, specifically including people who identify as LGBTQ+.

Abuse in LGBTQ+ relationships is an epidemic, and it's not being addressed in the national conversation as much as it should be. A 2011 National Violence Against Women survey found that 21 percent of men and 35 percent of women living with a same-sex partner experienced intimate-partner physical violence in their lifetimes, compared with 7 percent and 20 percent for men and women, respectively, who were in opposite-sex cohabitation. Transgender respondents had an incidence of 34 percent over a lifetime. My experience isn't a rarity. In fact, it's more commonplace than you would think, and it's a problem we need to solve.

I would always be very quiet about being an abuser. Most of my abuse was emotional or verbal, but there were some days where I would get extremely physical. No one else knew what was happening, other than Ray, but he wasn't in the room when it happened. No one was. I would have the fights in private, and I would do exactly what my father did: I would never touch my boyfriends' faces. I would only hit them in places that I knew they would have to hide. Ray would see the aftermath, and I would not lie to him about what I had done.

My fists weren't my weapons of choice—it was any object that was near me that could inflict pain. To be honest, I don't remember the exact ways I would physically abuse my boyfriends. Probably a defense mechanism—99 percent of that is blacked out in my memories.

What is clear to me is *why* I did it. The emotions around the abuse I administered still haunt me to this day. First, I think about my complex childhood trauma. I was living in a home where emotional and physical abuse were prevalent. The fact that it was never discussed in my home never allowed me to process my feelings around the abuse. As I continued through life, conflict and abuse felt normal, to some degree, in my subconscious. This led to a lack of accountability.

While I was abusive, I rationalized that my actions were somehow different than the actions of my father. I was better than him. I was different from him, which didn't allow me to see the reflection of him that was clearly staring back at me in the mirror. I also used the rationale that I was also hurting emotionally and mentally. In my mind, my own pain justified my hurting others. If I couldn't take accountability for my actions because I believed they were justified, then how could I stop?

The cherry on top of this disastrous sundae was the fact that I felt entitled. If my entitlement was challenged by my partner, that was not okay with me. I recall being out with one of my partners and a group of friends. He told them a silly story about my life that I believed should have been private. In hindsight, the story he shared about an evening where I felt a little sick after eating an Italian meal was comical and endearing. But in my mind, he betrayed me. How dare he share this embarrassing story about my life? With this betrayal came punishment.

I leaned over and grabbed his arm without anyone being able to see, and I squeezed it tightly. With a smile on my face, I whispered menacingly in his ear, "Wait till we get home." To the others, it looked like we were happily walking out of the party, hand in hand . . . but I was crushing his hand. The minute we got into the car, the emotional abuse started as I began insulting him. If he was silent and apologetic, normally it would not escalate, because somewhere in my mind I knew that I had broken his spirit and ruined his night.

But if for some reason he felt empowered to fight back, like he did that night, then I began hitting him. It breaks my heart to know that I acted like this. I was a product of the blueprint that I had seen in my household, but that is no excuse. It took me many years not only to ask for forgiveness from my partners but also to forgive myself.

Being gay, and having only straight family members or friends around me when I was growing up, and no gay public figures to watch, I never had relationships modeled for me. Now we're at a place where many more gay or lesbian couples are being seen in the media, so the public is getting a glimpse of how gay relationships work and how they can flourish. But at that point in the late '90s and early 2000s, there were no role models for me. As I was coming into my own as a gay man, I didn't have anyone to turn to and ask, "What does a gay relationship look like?"

Even today, I rarely hear anyone ask, "What happens when society tells you that it's okay for men to be aggressive with each other but you're a gay man?" For me the logic was, *I'm a man, you're a man, so it is acceptable for us to fight physically.*

I remember a boyfriend of mine, who I met while I was filming *The Real World.* We started dating after the show ended. This was the last relationship in which I was abusive.

One night we got into a big fight, and I was furious. By this point the media scrutiny from *The Real World* had slowed my physical violence, but I was still very aggressive and angry. I had a key to his apartment, and after the fight I let myself in. He wasn't home because he was out with a friend, which angered me even more. I thought, *How dare you not be here so I can finish the argument on my terms?* The more I waited, the more rage I felt, until it finally reached a boiling point and I began destroying everything in his room. I mean, I wrecked everything I could get my hands on.

If he were home, I'm sure I would have taken my rage out on him physically. My intention was to go in there and hurt him. Since he was not home, I broke every glass, broke his TV. I unleashed every bit of rage in me on his room.

I remember the boastfulness that I felt, similar to my father's, when I sat there after I was done and waited for him and his friend to come home. They saw the state the room was in and called the police. I encouraged it. I literally encouraged him to call the police—because I knew that if they came, they would see domestic violence between two men and dismiss it, and that would give me an even greater sense of satisfaction. That's exactly what the police did. They saw the room, talked to the both of us, and stated, "Well, you two guys just need to not hang out anymore."

I remember looking at my boyfriend with this arrogant smirk on my face that said, *I knew nothing was going to happen.* It was the same arrogant smirk my father would wear as he walked through life, because he knew no one was going to question his actions. Like my father, I knew I would get away with it. No one was going to take a fight between two men in an intimate relationship seriously enough to arrest me, so I continued the behavior.

That's a cultural belief that has to change. When domestic violence and abuse happen between same-sex couples, where's the training among police, firefighters, and nurses who aren't used to interacting with same-sex couples?

In a 2013 survey of gay and bisexual men published in the *Western Journal of Emergency Medicine*, 63 percent predicted that their interactions with law enforcement would be problematic due to experiences of homophobia and the anticipation of rejection and stigma from police officers. It's as if the violence gay people experience isn't valid or worth preventing in the eyes of the law.

It wasn't until my relationship with that boyfriend was ending that I started to realize I was morphing into my father. My boyfriend reminded me so much of my mother, in the sense that he was smart, loving, and supportive of my career. We had talked about all our dreams and our future together, and he had moved from Philadelphia to California for me, even though he didn't want to. My mother had also moved to Texas with my father, even though she didn't want to. My boyfriend went along with every part of my ride. Once he was gone, I realized I had to change.

The end of our relationship was the first time I didn't make excuses for my abusive behavior. The reason was because I was at such a low point in my life. The money had dried up from my being on *The Real World*, I wasn't working, and I was recreationally using cocaine pretty constantly. I just felt alone, other than the core people who never left me, like my best friend Ray, my other best friend Tre, and my sisters.

Me and my best friends Ray (center) and Tre in LA in 2010.
This is the day before I met Ian.

Me, Ray, and Tre in 2018, recreating the picture in Kansas City
while I was shooting season 3 of *Queer Eye*.

I realized if I ever wanted someone new to come into my life, and to have a healthy relationship, I needed to change. The first change I had to make was to stop being abusive. Being someone who is very decisive, the day my boyfriend disappeared out of my life, I went on Google and found an anger-management group in North Hollywood, California. A class was being held that night, so I rushed there as fast as I could. I walked into a small room with wood paneling and mismatched folding chairs. Maybe a dozen people were there, but I felt sad, confused, and alone. The person who was running the class was an older, white, straight man. When it was my turn to speak, he asked, "Did you abuse someone?"

I said, "Yes, my boyfriend."

Instead of dismissing it like others had, he said, "I'm glad that you're acknowledging that being abusive to your boyfriend is not right. Because being emotionally or physically abusive to a man is equally as bad as being emotionally or physically abusive to a woman."

It was the first time someone had acknowledged that my hitting another man was not okay, in the same way I would say that my father hitting my mother or sisters was not okay. It was the first time I ever said, "I'm abusive, but I don't want to be." I continued to go to that anger-management class almost every night for the next three months. I know it sounds crazy, but I had nothing else to do. I didn't have a real job. I didn't have a boyfriend. I wanted to spend the time working on myself.

I learned that abuse was a part of my DNA, and I constantly engaged in self-reflection in order to correct the behavior—to the point where I haven't been emotionally or physically abusive to any person since I finished the class.

In my twenties, I worked as a social worker, dealing primarily with LGBTQ+ youth. After my anger-management class, domestic violence became a big topic for me to discuss with them. I didn't want any boy or girl to feel that abusive behavior was okay to engage in.

My mother is now a healthy, strong, happy woman who is no longer married to my father. She made it out the other side. Even though I once repeated my father's actions, I, too, have come out the other side. I have learned to manage my anger, and I will never let my predilection for abuse rear its ugly head again. You can be in the darkness right now, whether being abused or the abuser, but you can get through it. In years to come, your story can be a testimony for someone else, so that they can learn how to get through it, too.

If you recognize the internal and external conflicts that support an abusive culture and make changes—seek out help, make amends, and forgive yourself—then things will improve. I'm thankful that I was able to recognize my behavior and correct it before it was too late. I can only hope that my story will inspire someone else to do the same.

chapter five

Coming Clean

have always had an addictive personality—and it developed long before I tried a single drug or drop of alcohol. I knew it from the relationship I had with porn during my puberty years. It was way too obsessive. Looking back on it now, there were all these red flags that every person around me should have probably seen, even if I didn't. But they didn't acknowledge it, because I don't think they had the language to do so.

If I had known better—and I really wish I had—I would have been able to look at myself more critically and say, "You have a predisposition for some of this behavior." I wasn't stupid; I knew I had a problem. It was that I didn't have the tools to know how to face it. I don't think there's a person who has gotten drunk and blacked out and said, "That's normal."

I had watched my father struggle with his own demons when it came to what I consider to be his addictions. The earliest memory I have of my father was definitely of him with a drink in one hand and weed or a cigarette in the other.

My father preferred alcohol and marijuana—and also Salem cigarettes, the ones in the green package. He would smoke weed first thing in the morning, and smoke again after he walked out of the house. I knew he smoked throughout the day because I could smell it, even if I didn't see it. He smoked weed in the house alone all the time. My mother didn't smoke or drink—I've never seen her tipsy in my life. But my father would smoke his Salem cigarettes, one after another, before moving on to the other vices he loved.

As the sun was setting, he'd grab a Budweiser or a Guinness, and start downing it. After that, he'd drink some concoction mixed with brown liquor. He would always drink with friends and relatives, so it seemed very social, like he was just having fun. But it was more than that. It would go until two in the morning consistently.

To be honest, I know that if he had not been smoking weed and drinking heavily, he would have been an amazing father 24-7. He already was in so many ways, when he wasn't battling his demons. He was adventurous—on a whim, he'd drop everything and go somewhere with us. He made great jokes, played good music. Still, as a child, I felt like there was always a moment when the alcohol and weed brought out the demons.

Having watched my father struggle with those demons, I think a lot of it came from the pressure of supporting his family and also the fact that he was Mr. Popular. I think that social pressure was a lot for him, because living up to the name Lucky can't be easy. It means everything always has to be good in your life.

What happens when things aren't good in your life? Even to this day, I know he still uses. I don't know if it is to the same extent as when I was a child. My father has always been what I would call a high-functioning addict. I know that others wouldn't use the "a-word." The message I received from him—as well as the media, and every single person around me—was that if you could still make it to work or school, and handle your business, then you weren't an addict.

When I was rushing home as a teenager to log on to watch explicit content on the Internet for hours upon hours, those were the first steps in a trajectory of addiction for me. I'm sure my family was aware that I was doing it. I never sat down and had a conversation with them about it, and they never walked in on me. But just like with most teenage boys, they knew what was going on but didn't address it. Instead, the joke was, "Well, he got his homework done. He's still making good grades." Or I would hear my father and friends joke, "Boys will be boys . . . this is natural." But it wasn't natural. It was obsessive.

I remember transitioning from my unhealthy obsession with porn at such a young age to my first time experiencing drugs, which was weed, at the age of sixteen. It's sad for me when I think about how I got drugs for the first time.

It was from my father's bedside table. I didn't have to walk too far. I literally just had to wait for him to leave the house and then go to his bedroom and take what I wanted. Dad had a brown tray that was organized beautifully. One corner of it had marijuana seeds and marijuana sticks. The other side had a large stack of crumbled weed, and then adjacent to both of those were rolling papers for the weed. It was always there. So on the day I decided with my best friend Ray that we were going to smoke weed after school, I knew it was my job to get it.

Ray and I had gotten to the point where we watched way too many videos from DMX and Method Man, big rappers from the early nineties. We'd watch videos of the Wu-Tang Clan where they were smoking weed, and we'd say to each other, "We have to try weed. It seems like the cool thing to do." We'd talk about it all day long, from the minute we got to school until the minute we came home.

I kept my father's constant use of weed a secret from everyone. I was embarrassed, to say the least. I also knew that I could get access to it in a heartbeat. I kept asking myself, *How do I say to my friend that I have access to weed without him judging me?* I always wanted to keep up an appearance that we were a somewhat normal family and lived in a normal house, but I knew that my home life wasn't normal. When you have a sixteen-year-old who has access to marijuana that's just lying around, something isn't right. I thought, *Okay, do I just grab some, and pretend I found it? Do I pretend that I have a guy I get it from, so I seem cooler? What do I do?*

On the day we decided to smoke weed for the first time, I opted just to say to Ray, "Hey, I'll meet you back at your house after school. I think I can get some." Of course, he didn't believe me. In his mind, there was no way that in our little suburban neighborhood, I could get some weed an hour after the school bell rang. But I could.

That day, I got off the bus, walked into the house, and paced around our living room for about five minutes. Up until that point, my after-school activities were homework and then watching videos. Suddenly my mind-set—the addict mind-set, where you get really consumed with thinking about one thing—had shifted to weed, weed, weed. *I want it. I need it. I've got to get this for myself. I've got to get this for my friends. I want to be cool.*

Even though I was worried my father would find out I'd taken from his stash, I told myself, *You know what? He's not even going to know it's missing.* I went into my father's room—I was always a latchkey kid and the youngest, so no one was home—and beelined for his brown tray of weed.

I sat on the floor next to the edge of his bed and took a piece of binder paper out of my backpack. Then I sprinkled a little bit of the weed in the center of it and grabbed some rolling papers. Because I had been watching my father roll his joints for so long, I knew exactly what to do.

Once I was done rolling the joint, I put it in my backpack and went to Ray's house. When I got there, he was like, "There is no possible way you have it." In disbelief, he watched as I pulled this tiny little amount of weed out of my backpack—I mean, it wasn't even enough to fill the rolling paper. I did that strategically, because I didn't want my father to know.

Ray looked at the packet with big eyes. "This is amazing," he said. Then, for the very first time, we got high.

And . . . I hated it! I hated every bit of it. I felt unclear. I felt like I was not in control of my body. I coughed uncontrollably, my eyes burned, my mouth was dry, and I felt horrible. During that entire first experience, I told myself, *You gotta pretend you like this.*

Side note: I live in California today, where medical marijuana is legal. I support people who are prescribed the drug and monitored by a physician. But I do believe there are dangers to children as well as to adults who use it excessively.

Back to that day . . . I may not have liked the weed, but Ray loved it. I wanted to continue to hang around him, so I decided that I was going to continue to like it as well. Even though I hated smoking, I kept taking small amounts of weed from my father over the next two weeks. Ray would always ask me where I got it from. Even though I had been worried about what he would think, I eventually confessed.

"It's from my father," I said, holding my breath.

Being my best friend, Ray didn't judge me. He just smiled and nodded. "Oh, I kind of figured you were getting it from your dad," he said. "He's a Jamaican Rasta. Of course he has it."

We laughed about it, and then we started to introduce it to other friends, because we wanted a bigger party. I remember Ray asked to come over to the house one day, so that he could see where I was getting the weed from.

At this point, there was another little secret that I had. I knew there was the small stash by my dad's bed, but I found out later where there was a much larger stash.

Inside the kitchen freezer of my home, there was a very large black plastic grocery store bag. Inside this bag was one of the biggest balls of weed you have ever seen in your life—about the size of a basketball—which my father kept there.

I thought to myself, *Well, if we're going to have more people doing this, I can't take the weed from his bedside for much longer. If I take it from this big ball, he probably won't notice.* So I started to gauge it with Ray, even though I was worried about what he would think.

As an adult, it seems so crazy to me that I grew up in a household with a basketball-size bag of weed in the freezer, but as a child, this was my life. I brought Ray over and thought, *You know what? If he's my best friend, he needs to know the truth. He needs to know every bit of me.*

I opened up the freezer door and showed him. Just like any young kid would be, he was amazed and thought it was the coolest thing on earth. In his freezer, he had steak, chicken, and leftovers from Thanksgiving, and here I had marijuana! He said, "Let's grab some." I carefully carved out a small piece that my father would not notice was missing, and I grabbed some rolling papers from his bedside table.

We met up with some other friends from our high school, and after that I became the supplier and the good-time guy, throughout high school, for weed. I became the person who was giving everybody weed and smoking weed, and it developed into something we did daily. We'd get out of school, and I'd get my homework done just fast enough so that we could start smoking weed.

This continued throughout high school, and nobody said anything to me about stopping. Not a single person. If I think back on it, at some point, my father had to have known that I was taking his weed, because I would come home stoned out of my mind. He had to have seen that basketball dwindling in the freezer, yet he never said anything to me. It just continued on.

By the time I got to college, I didn't want to smoke weed anymore. I knew that I was going to get rid of anybody who introduced weed into the conversation. I began removing potheads from my life—except for Ray, who would always be one of my best friends—because I didn't want them to pressure me into doing something I didn't enjoy.

That doesn't mean I was cured of my addictive behavior. Once I made it onto a college campus, drinking became the thing to do.

Drinking in college is often glorified in movies and encouraged through the party culture pervasive at many colleges and universities. It's seen as cool. In this kind of atmosphere, students are more likely to engage in unhealthy drinking activities, assuming it's a normal part of the college experience, but it shouldn't be.

I wish there would have been mandatory alcohol training when I was in school. I wish I had heard from every organization, from parents, from people around me, "It's not okay to drink this much. It's not a rite of passage." Maybe if I had understood how unhealthy alcohol was, I never would have started drinking in the first place.

The first alcoholic drink I ever had in my life was probably when I was six or seven. I was curious about it, so my father gave it to me. He would say, "I'd rather you tried it at home with me than do it out in public with someone else." Which is a really backward way of parenting, in my opinion, but that's what he thought.

When I got to college, my introduction to alcohol started fast. The first college party I went to, we pregamed before we left the dorm by taking a shot. When we got to the party, we were immediately handed a red cup filled with beer or liquor, and it would keep being refilled until I passed out or left the party. Everyone was doing it, and everyone around me was constantly drinking. So I figured, *As long as I get my schoolwork done, it could be a Tuesday night or a Saturday night—I'm going to drink.*

The next morning, I would always find myself asking, *Why? Why did I drink so much? Why do I keep doing this to myself? Why is this my norm?* Now I realize that many college students who binge-drink are just looking for a way to connect with other people and fit in. That was clearly the case with me, but this can be very destructive. The underlying pressures of being a college student—stress, loneliness, adjusting to a new life, depression, exhaustion—deepen and begin to create even more emotional and mental distress.

I would drink every single day, at every party. When I was eighteen, I went to the local liquor store with my friends. The man behind the counter leaned over and said, "You know, if you pay an extra twenty bucks, you can get whatever liquor you want." I handed him the money and he handed me back some bottles of hard liquor. That's all it took for me at eighteen to get all the liquor I wanted for myself and my friends.

I wanted to fit in so badly that I drank constantly. I felt pressure from friends and from myself, as I thought, *Well, this is what you do in college.* I was drinking everything from vodka to bourbon to whiskey, to a lot of beer, kegs of beer, trying to drink as much beer as I possibly could. I should have post-traumatic stress disorder anytime I see a red plastic cup.

Developmentally, my brain wasn't even fully formed. Cognitively and emotionally, I couldn't handle anything around me; I couldn't process it. I was dulling all the feelings I was having, and all the pressures I was experiencing, with liquor.

Again the narrative was, *I'm making it to class; I'm handling my business*, so I was able to think, *I'm not an addict! I'm not an alcoholic!* In hindsight, anybody who is drinking six to seven days a week consistently—you're an addict! In my opinion, you're an alcoholic!

As a society, we condone the rite of passage of drinking, because we know, as adults, that there's a lot of pressure put on college kids. But something needs to change. College students leave the family home and are tossed right into environments and told to be independent, to handle their own lives, to do everything. That's a lot of pressure.

I'll be honest: I didn't know how to cope with the pressure of life when I went to college for the first time. I know now that I coped by drinking, which continued for a long time. I remember going to class, but a lot of the rest was a blur, because I was drinking so much. Even my friends who didn't drink seven nights a week like me still drank three or four nights a week.

Once I graduated and moved to LA, I decided enough was enough with the drinking—and I did the same thing I had done in high school with weed. I'm very decisive, so I literally told myself,

I'm going to find friends who don't drink that much, because I'm exhausted. I don't want to drink anymore.

In the back of my mind, I'd always been aware of what I was doing and how it was affecting me, but it was so hard to correct it in the moment. My solution was to simply remove myself from those friends who drank excessively and find new friends who I would not have to drink with. Of course, this isn't the healthiest solution, because I was still avoiding the deeper issue—that the problem was me, not my circle of friends.

So just like after high school, when I got new friends who didn't smoke weed, after college I got friends who didn't like to drink. I didn't even drink that much on MTV's *The Real World*. I was never the one falling out of the club or going crazy (even though they supplied so much liquor in that house). I avoided the temptation of liquor by reminding myself of the bad feelings I had when I drank, and I didn't want to go back there.

In LA, Ray and I lived together. He and I have always been close, and we have always lived next to each other (still, to this day, we live only a few blocks apart). Ray still smokes weed as an adult, but he isn't a big drinker. When we moved in together, we decided we were going to create a new friendship circle with people who were more like us at the time.

But LA is a different beast! Yes, it is! I fell in with a new set of people, who said, "Oh, you should try ecstasy, it's really fun." I told them I didn't really know about ecstasy or Molly. But I wanted to hang around them, and they weren't big drinkers. So I decided I'd try ecstasy. My justification was, *Oh, these people only use ecstasy on Saturday nights when we go to a party. You take only one pill, you're not spending money at the bar, and you're drinking only a bottle of water throughout the night.*

I would think, *Look at me—I went from stealing weed from my father to drinking every night in college to now taking one pill and drinking water at a club. I am no addict! I'm in control. I know what I'm doing.* I was trying to convince myself.

Ecstasy became a Saturday routine for me. I would meet up with friends, and we'd go out to dinner and then go to a club. Before we walked into the club, I'd pop an E pill, which would slowly take over my mind and body. It's funny, I don't do these things anymore, but I think back with amazement to the fact that I had no idea what was in any of these pills. I don't think most people do. I wasn't getting it from a pharmacist who could tell me what exactly was in them—I was getting it from some shady guy named Ricky on the corner of La Cienega and Santa Monica Boulevards.

Not one of us would ever go to a doctor and let some shady person walk into the waiting room and give us random pills. You'd be like, "Hold on, what are you having me take? What's in this?" But not when it comes to drug culture! If Ricky hands you something, you're like, "Sure, I'll try it!" Funny how seamlessly drugs can cause us to relax our natural safety boundaries without being conscious of it.

Just like with all drugs, the euphoria I felt the first time I took ecstasy was quickly replaced by an upset stomach, dehydration, and headaches once the high had worn off. Soon enough, one ecstasy pill wasn't enough. I had to do two or three to get the same feeling I got the first time on one pill. If I was going to keep up with my friends, I needed more.

The first time I popped three pills, I was at a club dancing. It was amazing. A cool breeze from the air conditioner was blowing on me; I could see the smoke going up every time the DJ hit a different beat. I was in a kind of euphoria, loving the people all around me. Every time someone brushed up against me, my skin felt so good.

Then I remember dancing in the same club a few weeks later, after having just taken ecstasy. The smoke wasn't going with the beat anymore and ugh, the guy who just rubbed up against me was sweaty and gross. The drugs were no longer getting me high enough. I couldn't feel it anymore. It wasn't fun.

One time, I was at Atlanta Gay Pride with my other best friend Tre (just remember, "gay Tre, straight Ray"). He had never tried ecstasy before, so I told him we had to try it that weekend. I gave him one pill before we went into the club, and he said, "I don't feel it."

So I said, "Take another!" He said okay—trusting me.

For his first time, he was already taking two ecstasy pills. At the time, he had this shirt on that read, JOGGING WITH CHIP AND PEP-

PER. At about five o'clock in the morning, he was so high on ecstasy, he jogged around Atlanta. The ecstasy was keeping him up, and he didn't know what to do. We have joked many times afterward that if you get too high, you go jogging with Chip and Pepper.

As I write this, I'm thinking, *Who was I, and what was I doing to give my best friend two ecstasy pills on his first try?* It's sad. Even as all that was happening, I still stayed away from the harder drugs. I was always conscious enough to know that I didn't want to do anything harder because of vanity. I saw how crack affected people; I saw how heroin affected people. I saw how meth affected people's faces. I thought, *I'm too pretty for this; I'm not doing that.*

Those were the justifications I made in my mind—that those people were wrong, and I was right. My thinking in comparison to other addicts was *I am going to work; I am socializing; I am in control. Therefore, I am not like you. There's a difference between me and you. You can't cope with your life. I'm coping.*

But I was not coping with my life. When you're in the haze of any drug, alcohol, or addiction—you're not coping. I was avoiding my emotions, my issues, myself.

Ecstasy became an addiction, but within a year, I immediately stopped that one, too. Cold turkey. Just done. The reason is that I got to a place where I didn't want to have to take three pills to get high. Once again, I vowed to get rid of my circle of friends.

It was always my thought: *Once I get rid of these friends, I'll be better.*

In a heartbeat, I dropped them all.

Once that was done, I thought, *Okay, I'm free. I'm not drinking, I'm not smoking, and I'm not doing ecstasy. I'm good to go.* At this point, I was twenty-five. I'd gone through addictions with weed, alcohol, and ecstasy. Everybody acted like this was okay, because I was young and maintaining my life.

Then, four months or so after I quit E, I was introduced to my last drug ever—but it was the one that almost took me down. Tre and I met this whole new group of people who were very LA. They were young (or unwilling to let go of their youth). They were consumed with being invited to the hottest parties and knowing the coolest people. Having the most was never enough. If they had a new car, they needed a newer one; if they had the best clothes, they needed nicer ones.

At this point I had been on *The Real World*, so I had this influx of income. I was doing speaking engagements, I was getting paid to go to clubs—I'd get $10,000 cash to walk into a club.

I was doing these events over and over and over again, and I was exhausted. I was going from college to spring break to this club to that club, because everybody wanted to see the guy from *The Real World*. My boyfriend at the time said, "Well, I know something that we should try. Everyone else is trying it, and it can keep you up." I told him I'd do anything to stay awake.

I remember the first time I tried cocaine. I was sitting on my bed, looking at my computer (which is normal Karamo). I was typing away, doing work, and in walked Tre and my boyfriend, carrying this really big bag of white stuff.

I stared at it. "That's not real," I said. They assured me that it was. I was genuinely kind of excited, because I was so exhausted. *This could be fun. This is gonna keep me up. I'm in.* They brought it over to me, and like I was in a frickin' movie, I put my finger in it, then rubbed it on my gums. Why? I don't know. I had never tried cocaine before, but anytime people were given cocaine in movies or TV shows, they rubbed it on their gums. So that's what I thought I should do.

Immediately, my gums went numb. I knew then that it was real cocaine. I asked them why the bag was so big, and they said, "Well, we just ordered the biggest one." This was an eight ball—an eighth of an ounce, or 3.5 grams, of cocaine. This was a large amount . . . especially for first-time users.

I shut my computer screen and put on some music to get us in the mood—"What You Know" by T.I., because he talks about cocaine in the song. Then we just started getting ready for the clubs.

None of us had ever done cocaine before, so none of us actually knew what to do. We googled how to try it. We went through video after video: This is how you use it. This is how you sniff it. Don't use lower-denomination bills to sniff, because they have too much bacteria on them. Use a higher bill. Yes, we ran to the ATM to get a higher bill. That's drug logic for you: we didn't want bacteria up our noses, but rails of coke from God knows where was somehow okay! So absurd.

We got dressed and got high. I rolled up the bill and took a big sniff. It went up my nose, and . . . it burned so badly. There was a gross drip in the back of my throat. Why, in the movies, did people do this and it looked so fun? This was not fun. Just like with ecstasy, I also felt sick the next day. I felt sick every time I did it.

Every time I used cocaine after that, the first line I would do physically hurt. Why was I doing something that hurt, every single time?

The answer is that I was an addict. But I continued on, and cocaine became the drug of choice for me. I mean, I was the most focused I had ever been. That is the problem with addiction: when you find the drug that actually complements your personality, you've hit a new danger zone.

There's a line from the movie *Ghost* that jumps out at me—it's when Whoopi Goldberg says, "You in danger, girl." Anytime you find an addiction that matches your personality, you in danger, girl! In this case, I was in *real danger*. I had finally met my match. I was someone who wanted to be in control, to be aware, and I wanted to be able to do everything and be hyperfocused. Cocaine was like,

This is who you want to be? I'm going to give you all of that, and amplify it.

During the next few months, I was organizing everyone's parties. I was organizing life. I was going to work, still doing clubs and paid appearances from being on *The Real World*. I was laser-aware of every single thing. I became the person everybody knew they could count on when we were high, because cocaine made me so focused. It amplified my type A personality, and in the moment I loved it.

But I also hated the fact that I was wiping my nose constantly, because I had done so much coke that my nose was bleeding. I had a shooting pain in my head every day. After a weekend of bingeing, I would be depressed for three days straight.

I remember the first time that happened. We had our first weekend bender, and I couldn't do any paid appearances for work until Wednesday of that next week because I was so depressed. Cold and sweating in bed. I was just so sad, and I didn't understand why. Of course, I now know that it was because my body was going through withdrawal.

It got to the point that I set a fast-cash button on my ATM, so that any bank machine I went to, it would automatically pull out three hundred dollars, which I could give to my drug dealer to get more cocaine. It was an almost-every-day thing. I didn't like the feeling of how I was when I was down, so I kept it up. I had enough disposable cash to do so. It was crazy to be twenty-five, making $10,000 to walk into a club and stay for an hour and a half. What else was a young guy going to do but spend all this cash on cocaine for himself and all his friends?

My addiction wasn't something I hid. I knew it was wrong, but my mom and my sisters knew all about it (at this point, my father and I weren't talking). Ray was aware of it as well.

They were all against it, but no one stopped me. I don't blame them, because they didn't have the language. But this was a problem I didn't feel smart enough to stop on my own.

One New Year's Eve in particular stands out in my mind. Myself, Tre, and a girlfriend of ours were all going to a New Year's Eve party, with my mother in tow. The party was at a big fashion designer's house, and I was so excited that I had gotten invited. I asked my mom to come with me. My mother is someone I love to hang out with, even to this day. As I mentioned, she isn't a drinker or a drug user at all.

We were all getting ready and dressed, and I said to Tre, "Oh, honey, I'm going to order the bag." (We call each other "honey.") So I ordered the bag of cocaine. When it got to the house, we started doing it, with my mother waiting in the other room. Tre was all nervous, and I said, "Oh, honey, my mom knows."

Tre was in shock, because he respects my mother. He calls her "Ms. Grant," which is her surname. He said, "Ms. Grant knows?" I'm like, "Oh yeah. You think I'm lying to my family? That's not how I do it." To Tre, my response was typical Karamo—I can be brutally honest, so why wouldn't my mom know that I was using cocaine?

We got dressed, and everyone was looking lovely. I was high, feeling great; Tre was feeling great, and our girlfriend arrived. We ordered a taxi, because I thought, *I'm too high; I cannot drive.* It's funny how certain parts of me seemed to become more responsible, even while high. (I wasn't, it just felt like it.)

When the car pulled up, my friends and I got in the back, and my mom got in the front. Before we even got to the party, I pulled out the bag, and I started doing bumps of cocaine in the back of the car. My two friends stared at me in amazement like, *What the hell?*

I said arrogantly, "Oh, my mom knows. She's totally aware." I leaned toward the front seat. "Right, Mom?"

She turned around, and I'll never forget her face. Just disapproving. Her expression said, *I cannot believe this disrespectful child.* In that moment, what I really wish she had done was say, "Pull this goddamn car over. You're going home." But she wasn't able to do that with my dad, so she certainly was not going to have the language to do it with me.

Tre said, "Oh my gosh, I can't believe we're doing this." But that did not stop him, or our girlfriend, from doing a bump, too. We walked into the party, ready to have a good time. I reflect back on that now and think, *Wow. I was in the back seat of a car on New*

Year's Eve, getting high while my mother was in the front seat. What was wrong with me?

I know now what was wrong with me: I was addicted to cocaine.

That night went from bad to worse. When the clock struck midnight, I was inside the bathroom, shoving cocaine up my nose. I could hear everyone outside the door, counting down. I missed the countdown. I was in the bathroom by myself, dressed up nicely, getting high. Because I told myself that I needed one more bump beforehand, I ended up missing it.

But I wasn't thinking about what I was missing. All I was thinking about was getting high. When you're high, you don't want the party to stop. So as the night went on and my mother said she was ready to go home, I sent her home in a taxi. I was not even concerned about how she got home on New Year's Eve. How sad. There were so many people drinking and driving, and instead of focusing on getting her home, I just said, "Oh, get her a car; she'll be fine."

As I closed the taxi door, she looked at me with such sad eyes. She never expressed her disappointment, but she'd watched my father be this way. Now here was her only son, showing the same behavior.

But I had a party to go to. A friend of mine who lived in Hollywood told me that he had tons of cocaine at his place. I decided to go over there, because I couldn't reach my dealer and I wasn't ready for the night to stop. It was only three o'clock in the morning!

I got to the party, and there were people around and cocaine on the table, and I was like, *Great!* At twelve o'clock that afternoon, on January first, I was still up, with random people I didn't know, doing lines of cocaine. It was the worst New Year's ever. Chain-smoking cigarettes, doing coke, numb to everything, and looking at these strangers in the daylight, I couldn't believe that this was my life.

I kept using, and it just spiraled and spiraled. I still made it to work every day. I was a high-functioning cokehead. I would tell people at my MTV appearances about doing blow, and everyone would laugh it off, thinking it was funny. It became a conversation piece that people loved hearing about. No one encouraged me to quit, and I had no idea how to stop the train.

I was also forty pounds underweight, because the amount of cocaine I had done had wiped out all my body fat. I was too skinny and not looking cute. I've always been a muscular guy without trying—I'm almost six foot three, and my weight has typically fluctuated between 195 and 210 pounds. That's my area, but at that point I probably weighed about 170. I loved it at the time, because I was buying sample-size designer clothes and they fit great.

My mother and me in Paris in 2005. This is when I was doing drugs, and I had lost a lot of weight. I'm usually around 210 pounds, and here I was probably 175.

The boyfriend who had started this journey with me was also continuing to use. We had always said that we wouldn't try any drugs outside of cocaine, because those people were crazy. Then he started becoming erratic in his behavior—and when I say erratic, I mean he would start taping up the windows in the house with Scotch tape and be up all night doing it. Or he would go missing some nights. Something was going on with my baby.

The more worried about him that I got, the more I'd want to go out and do more cocaine. I discovered later on that he had been trying harder drugs. He had been trying acid, I believe. He was too embarrassed to tell me, because even though I was abusing drugs myself, I was quick to judge others who did the same. There are degrees to drugs—some have harder effects on you than others. In my mind, when I was doing coke at a club, I was being social; I was dancing, having fun. I wasn't like the people who did ketamine at the club, who were curled up on the ground in a k hole, or the meth or heroin addicts standing outside the club, picking at their faces. I wasn't like those people—I was better than them. Which is so stupid.

Eventually my boyfriend got on a plane and disappeared. I knew he was okay, because he was still withdrawing money out of my account. The money wasn't large amounts, like what you would need to pay the rent. Instead, it was small: $100 here, $150 there. I knew what was coming out was for drugs, but I was okay with that, because at least I knew that he was all right. (By the way, we've continued our friendship, and I'm happy to report that he got his life together and is doing amazingly well.)

Still, not having him with me sent me into a whirlwind of depression. Because I had lost the person who, at that point, had been the love of my life (although the real love of my life is the man I'm with now, in a healthy relationship that's drug-free, where we're communicating and raising two kids).

Once he disappeared, and my mental state started going downward, I began isolating myself. I remember the first time I finally did drugs by myself. I ordered coke, and I did it by myself in the house.

I knew that this meant I had a problem. Not that it wasn't a problem when I was doing it with others, too, but my needing to do coke alone really emphasized how bad it was. I had watched the American reality series *Intervention* for years, and every time I saw the person at their lowest point, they were by themselves in some corner. I realized: *Here I am, alone, emaciated, doing coke by myself in my apartment. There's just me and a bag of coke. That's all I have.*

I was depressed and having suicidal ideations. I wanted to die. I couldn't see a point in living. I was unhappy with traveling; my relationship with my father was done; I had lost my boyfriend. My family was mad at me because I was using drugs openly. I was lonely and alone. Life seemed like it was over.

So I attempted to kill myself.

My decision to attempt suicide is not something that happened overnight. If I'm honest with myself, I believe the dark feelings I had about myself began very early on in my life. I remember being in high school and feeling very sad and down based on something someone would say to me, or something that was going on in my family. It was never bad enough to keep me from interacting in life or make me want to hurt myself. But those feelings were always there, following me around like a shadow that was waiting to be acknowledged.

This continued throughout college and even during my move to California. Pockets of sadness would just appear in my life and sometimes feel overwhelming, but the majority of times they'd just feel like a nagging gnat flying around me. The thing about mental health that's similar to physical health is that you continuously have to check in with your mind, just as you check in with your body. You have to allow yourself the space to figure out what's going on with you so you can grow through it.

I never gave myself that space. I would happily talk about starting a new workout routine or diet but never about how I felt sad or depressed sometimes, how I was riddled with anxiety, or the fact that during moments of celebration, I felt like I wanted to be home alone by myself. Then there would be an occasion when something bad would actually happen. This could be an argument with someone in my life, a problem at a job, an issue with my finances, or myriad other situations. I would think to myself—never expressing it out loud—that I wanted to die just to escape it all. That harmful language would pop into my mind like chalk on a blackboard.

That's the thing about depression. As more bad things happened in my life, I felt more overwhelmed; I felt buried and alone. I seemed happy to the outside world because I always smiled through the mental and emotional pain, but when I was by myself driving home from work, I would have these random thoughts, like, *What would it be like if I weren't even here? Would anybody even care?* My mind was filled with questions that only led me to feel as if there was no hope in life.

It wasn't until I added both liquor and drugs to the mix that the chemistry with suicide was ignited—and caused all my issues to be amplified. The loneliness, anxiety, and sadness became one hundred times worse. The chemical toll that the drugs had on my already fragile mind exploded.

After doing drugs, I would be trapped in my room for hours upon hours, days upon days, just wanting life to end and thinking of possible ways to make that happen. It didn't start with me saying, *I'll kill myself.* It initially started as, *Well, if something bad happens to me, I deserve it.* This could be a car accident, or something where my heart stops beating from the drugs—anything of that nature.

Eventually, I realized that though I was playing Russian roulette with my life, the universe was not catching up to what I was hoping would happen to me. So I began to toy with small ways that I could hurt myself. Though I had these deep, dark feelings of wanting to leave this earth, it was only in moments of being intensely drunk or high that I actually felt that maybe I could take the steps to do it.

Somewhere deep in my subconscious, I was always worried about how others would find me if I were to commit suicide. I thought, *It would be unfair for them to walk in and see me hanging. It would be unfair for them to have to clean up the blood if I were to shoot myself.* That's where the idea of taking different pills came to my mind.

One day, I finally attempted suicide. It happened only once, but I am reluctant to go into detail about what happened next, out of the fear that I could give someone who is suffering from depression or having suicidal thoughts a plan to take their own life. Instead, I encourage anyone who is reading this to just remember that in those moments of darkness, there is hope, joy, and sunlight on the other side of these dark feelings. I beg you to take one step today, in this moment, and just ask for help from someone around you who you trust. Call an anonymous hotline that can provide you with help. The National Suicide Prevention Lifeline is 1-800-273-8255, and the Crisis Text Line offers free twenty-four-hour support when you text HOME to 741741. Or go to your local emergency room and ask to speak to a counselor or social worker about the feelings you're having.

During that dark time, I felt like my life was over. There was no point in existing. But I was given a second chance to accept support and to ask for help, and today I am living my dreams and am surrounded by love. Each day is a new day for me to continue to focus on my mental health. The same way that people get up and go to the gym to make sure their body gets exercised, or try to eat healthier, I continuously make decisions to make sure that my mind is strong—and that I am making sure I know I am worthy of living a good life.

After my attempt, my best friends Ray and Tre thankfully found me on the couch in my apartment, unable to breathe and wheezing for air. They immediately called an ambulance.

I was forced to go into the hospital for three to four weeks. During that time, I had to sober up. As I lay in the hospital bed that first day, a nurse came over to assess me. She looked me over with concern.

"Are you on anything?" she asked.

"Cocaine," I said weakly.

She leaned closer to me and studied my face.

"Sir, do you know you have a problem and we can help you?"

I shut my eyes in relief. It was the first time someone had said something like that to me.

It was also the first time someone said my addiction was bad. The first time someone said, "You need to stop." Finally, someone acknowledged I needed help. It took me trying to take my own life to get that help.

I stayed in the hospital for weeks, and that nurse called my mother and got her and my sisters there. My mother tells me the story of when she arrived, how she saw me in that hospital room and saw how skinny I was, and she broke down outside the door. That same nurse told her, "You have to be strong. He can't make it through this unless you believe he can make it through this."

I don't know who that nurse was, or where she is now, but that angel gave me the strength to stop. She gave my mother the strength to walk into that room and deal with her child lying in a hospital bed. After I got out of the hospital, my mother stayed with me for almost a month and tried to help me get my life back in order.

I wish this had a different ending, where I went to rehab and I stopped permanently. But rehab, to me, was a rich-people thing. We weren't rich, so I figured that wasn't for me. My money was gone (I blew through it, literally). My relationship with coke was not over yet. I was able to stop for a while, but then I relapsed.

Once I got out, Tre stopped using, too. It was easier for him to stop, because I don't think he really liked it. He had never gotten to the point that I had. I was dealing with so many demons. I was trying to cope with all kinds of conflicts in my life at that point, like not being able to talk to my father anymore, and being stressed about where my life was going, my sexuality. The image people had of me my entire life was that of a person confidently going after his dreams, but I was not going after them.

When I relapsed, it was maybe eight months after I had stopped and I was back on my feet. That was when I learned, at the age of twenty-five, that I was a father (which you will read about in an upcoming chapter). I had a son in Houston whose existence I didn't know about until I was served papers seeking back payment of child support.

That news, as you can imagine, shocked me into delirium, and I needed something to cope. I didn't know what to do with it and couldn't handle the pressure. I needed a fucking bump of cocaine. The weekend I found out I was a father was when I started going to the clubs again.

After a long two days of waiting, the day arrived when I was to fly from Los Angeles to Houston to meet my son. At five thirty in the morning, I was going through security. As I was pulling everything out of the pockets of my army-green cargo shorts to put in the tray—my wallet, my keys—I realized I had also pulled out a bag of cocaine I'd been carrying around.

As I watched, that bag of cocaine started going down the conveyor belt. I was about to go from LAX to jail, on the way to meet my son. A woman in security saw my panicked face and thought I was afraid to fly. "It's okay, baby," she said, waving me through. "Go on."

I was so scared. I had worked so hard to get clean, how was I going to tell everybody that I'd relapsed? How was I going to tell everyone who was so proud of me that I actually hadn't gotten my life back together? Even though they weren't there for me before when I was asking for help, they were there now. They were applauding me. Now I was back at it.

I was so exhausted that I just accepted it. Like, *Fine. Maybe this should just be done*. With my heart pounding, I walked through security. My tray made it through. They didn't see the cocaine. Afterward, the guard smiled and said, "That wasn't that bad, was it?"

After that ordeal, a sane person would have tried to throw the bag of cocaine away to avoid any more issues, but not me. I got all my stuff off the conveyer belt, ran to the bathroom, and finished the baggie in a bathroom stall. I'd made it through that pressure situation, so I decided to celebrate. All my previous worries about not being clean went right out of my head.

When I got on that plane to go meet my child for the first time, I was high. When I got to Houston, my sister Kamilah could tell that something was wrong. It wasn't like I told her anything. It wasn't like I was disheveled. Still, she just knew—it was that sister intuition. I was staying at her place, and when we arrived at her house, she turned to me and said, "You're not fucking coming down here and doing that shit. Nope. No, you are not."

It was the first time someone in my family took a hard stance about what I was doing. "You have a kid now," Kamilah told me. "This is not happening. If you're staying here, you're not fuckin' doing this shit." She became my mother, watching me like a hawk throughout my stay. It was her watching me that made me stop the behavior.

The biggest thing was that she helped me figure out what was wrong with me. She was like, "You're an addict. This came from Daddy. This is not anything you can do by yourself. You need support." When she said that, I felt so happy. She put her foot down and said, "Before you meet this child, you need to get yourself together."

Kamilah's a PharmD, which is a doctor of pharmacy, and she

told me what goes into the drugs I was using. She illustrated to me clearly all the chemicals that got mixed in the drugs and how I should never be putting them in my body. The minute I learned from her that crack and cocaine were the same thing, I realized that I was a crackhead (and also that my judgments of other addicts were unfair, because I was in the same boat).

Kamilah, Mommy, and Nedra. My loves, my support through everything.

Cocaine is a powder that's frequently snorted, while crack cocaine is a version of cocaine that's mixed with baking soda so it can be smoked. Kamilah showed me literature and videos about it, illustrating exactly how it was affecting my brain and my moods. She shocked me, but she also educated me. I wish I had gone to rehab, but luckily, with her support, I made it out a different way.

By the time I met my son Jason about seven weeks after I arrived in Houston, I was back on the right path but also had gotten the tools to finally figure out how to combat this internal conflict of addiction I was battling with. These included being honest with myself, developing better coping skills, and learning what my trigger was. Figuring out my trigger—what pushed me to want to do drugs or drink—was key in taking responsibility for my own actions, and mine was feeling pressure.

To this day, I have to manage the amount of pressure I have in my life. There are moments where I'm still like, *Well, maybe if someone offered it to me, I might try it.* That's the addictive personality in me.

The cast of *Queer Eye* and I were recently invited to present at the seventieth annual prime-time Emmys. It was such a big honor, but at the time, I was being pulled in a million directions with my career, my kids, and my schedule. I rented a fancy suite at the Ritz-Carlton to get ready, and I invited people over. The hotel upgraded me to the biggest room they had. It was amazing. I was about to go to the prime-time Emmys for the first time.

As we were all getting ready, one of my friends offered me cocaine. Trust me, I was stressed beyond words at that point. Nobody would know if I tried it. My kids were in the other room. My fiancé was in the other room. Immediately I had to manage myself and say, No. *The reason you're even contemplating this is because the pressure is too much for you in this moment, and you want to escape it.* I had to check in with myself, because now I understand what my trigger is.

I said to my friend, "I'm sorry, you have to leave." I went to the bathroom, sat down on the edge of the tub, and just tried to breathe. I had to tell myself, *You're stressed, but channel the stress into working hard and enjoying this moment.*

As I look back on my life, I see that all my addictions were caused by pressure. I escaped from the pressure of wanting friends and the need to be liked in high school by using weed. In college, I escaped from the pressure of doing well in school by using alcohol. I did the same thing with ecstasy and with cocaine. When I look back, I understand that I always want to use when I feel pressure and when I'm working my hardest. To this day, I still have to manage it.

People grappling with addiction or any obsession will say that it's like a big bear that's hugging you and you want to get loose from it. You don't want to be in its claws, because it hurts. That's the only way I can explain the picture of it—a bear, a violent creature that is holding you tightly. Its claws are digging into you, but you don't know how to escape.

Now I know that step one is to ask for help. It's also understanding my trigger—which became a tool I used to take responsibility for my actions and find the courage to say no to my addictions. I do wish I would have been able to go to rehab or see a drug counselor, but I didn't know how then, nor did I have the money I assumed it would cost. Luckily, I have finally conquered this conflict and am living a healthy life, but I still have to take it one day at a time.

chapter six

A Dream Deferred

When I was a kid, I used to wake up early in the morning on the weekends, before anybody else. I'd grab the blue sheet off my bed, run into the kitchen, and fill the thermos from my Sesame Street lunchbox with Kool-Aid. (Side note: I still love my sugar, which the guys in the Fab Five tease me about. I'm allergic to chocolate, so on the set, I eat a lot of Twizzlers, Skittles, and Starbursts, and I drink a lot of Coca-Cola and Sprite. Tan has a sweet tooth, too—he likes his desserts. The others are like, "Let's eat healthy," and I'm like, "Ugh, get a life!")

With my sheet and thermos I would head for the TV in the living room, which was the only one that we had in the house.

I would pop in a VHS tape of the Spike Lee movie *School Daze*, which was one of my favorites. It showed the experience of twenty-something African-American kids on a college campus, but all of that was lost on me. Instead, I became fixated on a scene in the movie that took place during homecoming. The four girls who were the antagonists of the movie, because they were the pretty mean girls, performed at homecoming in these silver-and-black dresses.

Tisha Campbell-Martin, from *Martin* and *My Wife and Kids*, was the lead singer in the group. The homecoming scene opened on a dark stage. The spotlight came down, and then they went into this seductive dance routine in these tight dresses. I would tie my bedsheet around me and dance to that routine with my Kool-Aid in my hand. All I knew was that I wanted to be Tisha Campbell-Martin in that show.

It was probably the most magical thing I had ever seen in my life. I looked at them and thought, *That is who I want to be. Not a woman, but this is what my career has to be. My career has to be me, onstage, making people scream, making people excited. Being glamorous.* I would rewind that same scene, over and over again, because I wanted to be that person who got rewound, over and over again. To this day, I still know that whole routine.

As I got older—and figured out, first, that being a mean-girl diva in a movie is not really a career you can choose—I kept wondering what I wanted to be. That was a question that was constantly asked in our household, especially because my parents were immigrants.

It was always, "What do you want to be?" My parents came here to make sure that we had opportunity and a better life. We heard it often, to the point where I had anxiety around the idea, even at a very young age. Every time I was asked that question, I would get a knot in my stomach. I knew that I had to formulate some answer quickly to appease all the adults around me.

I knew if I said, "I want to be like the woman on TV who dances," that was not going to be an okay answer. It had to be based in reality, and there were certain careers that my parents knew weren't for me. Like, if I had said I wanted to be a doctor to appease them, they would have seen right through that and been like, *Girl, please*, because if I see blood, I scream and run.

If I had said I wanted to be a truck driver, that wouldn't have worked, either, because I'm one of those people who gets in a car and will go to sleep in five minutes. The moment I start getting rocked like a baby in a car, I'm out. (Even to this day, when we are driving to help one of our heroes on *Queer Eye*, it's a struggle for me to stay awake.)

At one point when I was in the fifth grade, I did tell my parents that I wanted to be a dancer. The reason I said it was because my sister Nedra was on the drill team. Drill team is different from cheerleaders, in the sense that they don't cheer, and they're not interacting with a crowd; they usually perform choreographed dances at halftime.

I remember watching Nedra practice every single day. I would be in the house, learning her routine, just like I had with Tisha Campbell-Martin's routine from *School Daze*.

Nedra still jokes about this—I would be at her games on the sidelines, doing all the routines with the girls, because I had memorized them. I would be at the dining room table, doing my homework, just enamored with watching Nedra practicing in the living room. I loved the sparkle and the glitz of her costumes. It's no wonder I'm in a sparkly bomber on TV these days. All these things play into *Who is Karamo?*

When I told my parents that I wanted to be a dancer, I was shut down immediately and told, "That's not a real job." It's funny how parents, when they're doing what they think is best, can also stifle a child's dream. As a parent myself, it's one of the things I'm most conscious of—how my words can either be daggers that kill something my children love and dream about, or how they can have the power to truly uplift them.

My parents weren't malicious when they said that I couldn't be a dancer. As an adult, I know that their response was most likely, "Oh, Karamo, think about something else." But at the time, I received their feedback in my young mind as "You want to be a dancer? What are you, a sissy? That's not a career for you! That's stupid!"

That feeling stayed with me. It affected every club I joined in middle school, high school, and college. I always figured I needed to do something that was going to be the opposite of dance. So the first club I ever joined that I was really exceptional at was FBLA, the Future Business Leaders of America, which I joined in junior high and stayed in throughout high school.

I excelled because I was a quick problem solver and could talk to anyone. I was like, *Oh, if this is what business is, I'm going to do well in this. Here we go.* After that first meeting, I came home and told my parents that I wanted to be a business leader—not giving them anything specific—and I immediately saw the excitement on both of their faces.

It's funny how certain things in your mind stick with you, because I was thinking, *Wow, that made them happy.* As human beings, we like validation from other people. If you say something and someone smiles or is happy, you start to repeat that behavior, because you know you're going to get attention. That's how we all are. We often develop into who we are based on how people interact with us, but as we get older, it's our responsibility to grow based on how we feel about ourselves. We must make sure that we are not letting others' opinions of us dictate who we are or who we become.

Nevertheless, the minute I saw my parents' joyful reactions when I told them what I wanted my future career to be, I thought, *Whatever this is, this is where my career needs to go.* That led to me joining the Student Government Association through middle school, high school, and even college. I joined every school patrol—

anything that had to do with leadership. I was training myself to be a leader, because it was a career my parents were not questioning.

But then I had another moment similar to seeing Tisha Campbell-Martin in *School Daze*. I was in tenth grade, and I was at the table doing homework. (Do you notice how I'm always at a table doing homework? Homework was big in my life. That's another thing about immigrant parents. It was like, homework! Homework! Homework! Even when I didn't have homework, I had homework—writing assignments and summer reading. So. Much. Homework.)

I was doing my homework, and the TV was on, because I have always been one of those people who can work with a lot of noise around me. I think that quality is also what makes me such an empathetic listener, even on camera. There's so much emotional connection between me and the heroes on *Queer Eye* because even though there's a crew of twenty people around and between us, I can tune all that out and just listen and focus. That goes back to my days in school—where I'd study with tons of noise in the background.

As I was studying, all of a sudden I heard this high-pitched voice on the TV that sounded like a man but at the same time didn't sound like a man. Without looking up, I immediately realized that the speaker had to have been gay, because they were saying something like, "Let's get up and dance, honey!"

I looked at the TV screen. It was RuPaul, doing his opening monologue on his VH1 daytime talk show. It was like someone had put a lasso around my neck and was slowly drawing me in. I felt like I floated over the table and directly in front of the TV. You know when you see a kid who's way too close to the TV, looking up at it, wide-eyed? That was me.

I had never, ever in my life seen something like this. At this point, I was completely aware that I identified as a gay man, but I had never seen black gay men anywhere in the media. Though I never once dressed in drag, I knew that underneath RuPaul's costume and performance piece, there was a gay black man. And he had his own daytime talk show!

I was hooked. After seeing that first show, I would run home every single day to watch RuPaul. It was the most groundbreaking thing to me. It was at that moment I realized, *No, no, no—that's what I want to do. That is what I have to do. Connecting with others like this is what I was born to do.*

When you have a moment of clarity that young, and you get to a place where you know what you're destined to do, it's an out-of-body experience. Even as a child, I was watching RuPaul, but I was also looking at myself, knowing, *That is my job.*

RuPaul would tell his guests on the show, "You've got to love yourself, honey." He'd be giving them this inspiration, and I was inspired, too: whenever the audience would get excited by something, I'd scream along with them. He would have these fun conversations with his guests, but it would be more than that, because he had a very strong way of making people feel seen and validated. As a young child, all of that resonated with me so much.

It was because of RuPaul that I then started to take my mom and sisters' VHS tapes of their soap operas—they watched *General Hospital* and *All My Children*—and record episodes of Phil Donahue and Sally Jessy Raphael over them, so that I could come home to watch and study these daytime talk shows (after I had done my homework, of course).

I don't know if I even had the language to describe the job as being a talk-show host. I just knew that I wanted to be that person, talking on TV. (And I'm still working toward that goal of having a talk show!)

I was enamored with Phil Donahue. He could dissect a conflict quickly and give clear facts about it in a way that wasn't judgmental. He could talk and relate to anyone, and throughout, he maintained a great sense of humor. Kids today don't even realize that the audience participation talk-show format was created by him. I have so many kids who tell me that they want to be a television host. I encourage them and tell them they can do it, but I also tell them to make sure to study the people who came before them.

The fact that these talk-show hosts were able to have these critical and culturally relevant conversations was just exciting to me. I would go to school the next day and engage in these same sort of conversations with my classmates. In my mind, it was like I was practicing for my own talk show.

In tenth or eleventh grade, I'd bring people together in the lunchroom who had been fighting, like two best friends or a girl-friend and boyfriend. I'd gather people around and say, "Hey, every-body. So we all know that Daniel is being accused by Jessica of cheating." I'd get this *Ooooh* from everyone around us, and then I'd say, "Jessica, tell everybody what's going on."

Or I'd bring up topics for discussion for my "studio audience." I did that all the time. I'd think, *Everyone's watching, they're super excited, these people are pouring out their guts in front of everyone. I don't know how to manage this, but I don't care! There's a crowd around me!*

Even though I had these secret fantasies of being a talk-show host, I never told my family about it, nor any of my friends. My parents had already told me that dance was not an option, so TV was definitely not going to be an option, either.

It's ironic, because my father had quit his job as an accountant to pursue his dream of being a radio host (and actually ended up being a late-night DJ on a Houston radio station called KTSU, 90.9, when I was in middle school). Yet he still made me feel as if a career in entertainment was not a career. As an adult, I understand why: he took his baggage, and the baggage that he had received from everybody else, and he put it on me. Because everyone had told him no, he didn't have the language to tell me yes.

As he was struggling to support his family, I'm sure that all he was thinking was, *Well, I don't want my child to struggle as he sup-ports his family one day, so entertainment can't be an option.*

He encouraged me to pursue other careers, and I did what

would make my mother and father happy. I wanted to be in theater and the film club at school, just to practice, but there was no way that I could do any of that stuff, because I knew that I would have to come home with a permission slip for them to sign. If that said anything other than Student Government Association, FBLA, National Junior Honor Society, or sports—all of which I did—I thought I was going to be greeted with a "You can't do this."

It was in about tenth grade that I really started struggling with this career idea. Even now, when I think back to that time, I get anxiety in my stomach, because it's when we started to deal with SATs, ACTs, and college visits. The question on the college application and from the school counselors was always, "What do you want to be?" I felt sick every time I had to go in and talk about it. I knew what I wanted to be, but it just wasn't an option.

When I was in tenth grade, my school started a new club called Peer Counseling. I visited the club meeting one day as a fluke, because a girl I was hanging out with was joining the club. On that first day, I walked into the classroom and listened to the teacher talk about what the club did and how it was going to help other students. They said our duty was to be a peer who students could talk to about their issues, and that we would help get them to the appropriate counselor or teacher they needed. We were their hand to hold and ear to listen.

Even though I know my job was to help other students, the only thing I heard was, "This is the training you need to be a talk-show host." What that teacher was saying to me sounded a lot like the episodes of Phil Donahue and Sally Jessy Raphael and Ricki Lake that were recorded on my VHS tapes. "You're going to listen to people, and they're gonna tell you about their problems. And you're going to help them," she repeated.

It took me not even three months to become the lead peer counselor.

When I started to do it, I realized I had the gift of being a really empathetic listener. I was able to connect the dots in a way that a lot of the people in peer counseling couldn't do. I could quickly ask, "Where did this behavior start? What happened? How can we solve this problem?" and then identify solutions. So I rose rapidly in the club ranks. Seeing students figure out their own lives with my guidance brought me a huge amount of joy, even as I was confused about my own life.

When you have a young high school girl who's crying over her boyfriend and you help her realize that she is worth more than anything he's ever said and that she doesn't need him, and she walks out of the room feeling empowered, that's a rush.

When you see somebody who is "broken," it's like doing a puzzle. Have you ever seen those videos of people doing Rubik's Cubes where they do it really quickly, and all of a sudden, all the sides match? That's the feeling I get every time I help someone, and it started way back then.

Right away, I went home and thought, *I want to be in a space where I help people.* Then I started to learn words like "psychiatrist" and "psychologist" and "social worker."

Well, when my parents heard all these job titles, they said, "Yes! Oh my gosh, yes! *Yes.*" After that, everywhere we'd go, it was, "Karamo's going to be a psychologist one day!" Parents love to tell other parents what their child is going to be one day, and they would brag about it. I felt good, because not only was I making them happy, but I also found something I legitimately liked to do. It was part of me, who I naturally was.

So when I got to college, I fell right back into the pattern of what I knew was the "right" path for me. I majored in business. I joined student government. I was voted class president. I did peer counseling on campus. I became the presidential ambassador. I was on the homecoming court. I did all these things that put me in a position of leadership.

With some members of the student government in college.

Homecoming court was not what we know traditionally—as in, being voted homecoming king or queen—but was more of a way to be a leader and a liaison between students and faculty, or students and people who were visiting the college. We had to be able to talk about the school in a way that was very clear and articulate.

Me with the homecoming court at Florida A&M University. We were ambassadors of the school, so we'd walk around the games in full suits or tiaras.

We were being trained to be these sorts of dignitaries. (Although, side note, the reason I joined the homecoming court was because of Tisha Campbell-Martin. That's never left me. When I found out that the women got to perform but the men had to stand stoic in the back, it tore me up.)

Leadership just became what I was going to do, along with being a social worker. Still, it felt like a piece missing—and it was the vanity piece. I wanted to help people, but I also wanted people to know who I was. I ran for student government; I was popular on campus. I did this because I wanted to be seen, validated, and at the forefront. I didn't want to just fade away into the background.

It was in college that I got introduced to politics. The first publication I was ever in was the *Famuan*, which was our campus newspaper. I was on the cover, which read, "Karamo Brown: Youngest Candidate for City Commissioner of Tallahassee." This was because I decided one day, after doing a peer-counseling event where I was helping people, that I was going to run for office.

I had been reading about how the two main campuses in Tallahassee, Florida State University and Florida A&M University, made up 90 percent of the constituency in the city—yet all the legislation at that time was against students. They had the audacity to fight against us? It made me angry.

It was because the incumbent in town was being "a jerk"—

that's how I put it in my speech (I have better words now). I figured I could galvanize all the people on my campus and on the neighboring campus of Florida State to vote for me if I ran for office. That way I could still help people and do all the things that the current city commissioner didn't do, but people would know who I was.

It immediately spread across the campus that a student was running for office. Getting involved in politics was a mix of all my passions. I was too far into my major at this point to change it to political science, but I didn't care. I was going to run for office anyway.

As I started going to these events, I soon realized that I wasn't prepared enough to actually run against this man. When you're running for office, you have to really know what you're doing and saying, and have a clear understanding of how you can help people on a larger scale than just having a one-on-one conversation. It was the first time I really had respect for politicians.

So after about four months of running, I withdrew my candidacy and I went back to helping people on a one-on-one basis instead. As I matriculated through college, it was about social work, psychotherapy, and helping people get to a place where they understood their lives and what they were going through. Even though the dream of being on television had never, ever left me, I'd done everything that was expected of me. Now my parents could say, "Oh, look at our son, he's a social worker; and look at our daughter, she's a pharmacist; and look at our other daughter, she's a counselor."

I resented them in a sense, because I hadn't fulfilled my dreams. But I had no idea how to engage on this path of going into television. The only thing I knew to do was to go where the industry was—then maybe somehow I could find an entry point and move into it.

I decided to relocate to California. I didn't tell one single soul I was doing it. I was scared that if I did, they would fight against me going, and I might give up this one last shot I had to fulfill my dream.

I packed up my green Jeep Cherokee, which had dual engine exhausts and was the loudest thing you could imagine. On the last day of school in Florida, I got on I-10. On the way, I stopped in Texas for maybe a day. My family thought I was coming to visit, which I did often, and then I'd go back to Tallahassee to start some sort of job.

Because I was so self-sufficient no one questioned me. It wasn't until I was leaving that I told my sister Kamilah I was moving to California. She thought I was joking. I wasn't. I got in my truck and continued on I-10 all the way to Los Angeles, where I didn't know a single soul.

Throughout college, I worked at a Holiday Inn—first as a front-desk agent, then as the front-desk manager, then as night manager. Being the night manager and the night auditor was the only way I could go to school and still maintain a job (and buy the speakers for my Jeep Cherokee).

I'd used that time to study through the night, to keep up with my schoolwork on top of all the activities I was doing. It was quiet time for me to focus. I had trained myself for five or six years to stay up half the night and still be able to function with only four hours of sleep.

When I got to Los Angeles, I parked my car at a Crowne Plaza in Beverly Hills, which was a safe space. I thought, *Well, if nothing else, I have discount points, so I can go in there and get a room while I figure things out.* I'd been sleeping in my car on the way to California, because I couldn't afford to stay in hotels. I went into the lobby, and a man asked if he could help me. I told him I had just moved there, and as we started talking, I found out that he and I were both Masonic brothers. The Masonry, which I joined when I was nineteen, is one of the oldest fraternities in the country. It's all about service and giving back to the community. I figured they were like-minded people I could spend time with, and I had also read an article that many US presidents were Freemasons. There's all this secrecy around the Masonry, too. I heard all these wild stories about their secret meetings. (Then you get in and find out it's a bunch of old guys reading the Bible.)

Me as a Mason in 2002, doing a community project where we were building something. You can see I have a Masonic shirt on.

He asked me if I needed a job, and I said, "I actually do."

He then asked if I knew anything about the hotel business.

"Funny you should ask," I told him. "I do."

He gave me a job, and because he was the general manager, and a fellow Masonic brother, he let me stay in the hotel for three weeks for free while I found a place to stay.

So I became the night manager at that Crowne Plaza, which is now a Marriott. I remember getting off work and I would go on top of this parkway that overlooked the hills to watch the sun set, and I would sit up there, dreaming that one day, I'd be on television. I would sit on the hood of my car, thinking, *I can do this. I don't know how, but I'm gonna figure it out. I'm in LA, and that's half the battle.*

Working at the front desk at the Beverly Hills Crowne Plaza hotel in 2003. Kids today may not know that thing attached to the phone is called a cord.

My very first night of working at the Crowne Plaza. I was scared shitless. I'm in California, working at the front desk, ready for my new life. Somebody there should have *Queer Eye*'d me on how to tie a tie.

At this point, the only talk-show host who was doing anything remotely close to what I wanted to do was Oprah Winfrey. But she was (and is) a megastar. There was no way I could be her. I could dream big, but not that big. Part of the reason I said that to myself was because I still heard the voices of my mother and father telling me that this wasn't a real career.

I got an apartment on the day that I had to move out of the Crowne Plaza, so I was cutting it close. I got it from this sweet lady and couldn't believe she rented it to me, because it was a big, gorgeous apartment in a luxury building, and the rent was so cheap. It was a two-bedroom apartment, and my best friend Ray moved out to LA to become my roommate. (My other best friend Tre moved out to LA four years later, and he still lives in the same apartment to this day, because he took over my lease when I moved out.)

Then I got a job at an organization called the Brotherhood Crusade in South Central. It was the first job I got out of college besides the Crowne Plaza, and they needed people who could do counseling for young kids and also do engagement with the community. I thought, *This is awesome! I'll work with young kids; it's a predominantly African-American organization . . . I got it.*

While I was working there, some of the kids in my program started getting arrested because they were watching a show on MTV called *Pimp My Ride,* which was hosted by the rapper Xzibit, where they took average cars and turned them into over-the-top ones. My kids were stealing cars to try to make their own cars better. Being a young activist, I thought that to save my kids, I needed to get that show off the air. That was the way my mind worked. Being twenty-two and idealistic, I decided to get together some community members to go protest MTV and request they be more responsible for what they were teaching.

I stayed up all night. I created posters. I made a PowerPoint presentation. I was like, "We're gonna save our children. Young kids, who are your main demographic, are getting locked up in juvie. There's a pattern here that is affecting kids of color, kids who are disenfranchised and don't have any money, and this show is glorifying that all you have to do is take from something else and put it on your car. MTV needs to know that this is wrong."

I called people from the local news and got them to come out, and we went down to MTV Studios in LA and started protesting. A woman came out and asked who organized it.

"I did!" I told her. "And this is wrong!"

She said, "We want to talk to you."

I said, "Okay, well, let me get my boyfriend." (He was a little older than me, and I needed somebody older than me to come with me for support.)

She said, "You have a boyfriend? We want to meet with you. Come back in two days."

I went home, thinking that I was about to get the show canceled—that I was about to effect change. I prepared all these talking points for the media.

Two days later, I met with them and they told me, "We brought you here because we think you're a dynamic character, and we want to put you on MTV's *The Real World*." Four weeks later, I got cast on the show. It was probably the fastest casting in the show's history, and it was because they saw an "angry" (not passionate, educated, or rebellious) black guy protesting with his boyfriend outside of MTV.

The interviews I had with the producers were easy for me, because I would just answer their questions thoughtfully. Because I'm an open book and never tried to hide who I was or what I'd gone through, it was easy for me to talk about my life. That's what they want on reality television: someone who can talk.

People think reality television producers cast characters, but it's the exact opposite. They don't cast characters; they cast people, and people are multilayered. Anytime someone goes into a casting and they try to be the character of the oversexualized girl, or the bro-y guy, they never get the show.

That might be the part of your personality that's highlighted in contrast to someone else, but they're not casting that one piece. They don't know how you're going to be interacting with other people; they have to make sure that all parts of you come out and show that you have depth. If you're going, "I'm the party girl; I only love to party," then they're thinking, *Well, she has no depth.*

A month and a half after that protest, I was on a plane to Philadelphia. We were going to shoot *The Real World* with seven strangers. I was so excited. I was this child who had just been told I could be on the hottest reality show of the time. I jumped on the opportunity without thinking. I saw it as an honor and thought that I would have a national platform to discuss issues like race and sexuality.

Being on MTV was, in my mind, a stepping-stone for what I wanted to do—but it actually became one of the darkest times of my life. I got in this house and immediately, every single issue that I had was getting produced for the world to see.

Everything I wanted, everything I'd been through, and every part of my personality was exposed. There's a reason they cast me on that show: I was not the typical young man. I was gay. I supported religion. I had issues with my father. I was Caribbean. I was very outspoken about race and politics. I had been an excessive drinker. In other words, I was a recipe for reality TV.

I felt like their direction was, "Let's take a kid who has all these issues that he's trying to work through and doing a pretty good job of solving, and expose them for the next five months. We're gonna put him in a house with people who are gonna constantly talk about his issues, alongside their own."

It was a roller coaster ride that I wanted to get off badly, because it was so painful. I thought to myself, *This is why my parents told me I shouldn't be a dancer or on TV.* They weren't trying to kill my dreams. They were trying to protect me, because I wasn't built for this.

There was a bench outside our *Real World* home in Philly. I would leave the house to lie on that bench, curled up for hours upon hours, because I just couldn't handle what was going on inside. After a while, my roommates and producers would make jokes—they would call it my "homeless bench." I went there because my spirit was being crushed, day in and day out. Any time I had a conversation, it was misconstrued.

I had an African-American castmate, for example, and everyone thought I had an issue with interracial dating because she was dating a white guy. I never cared about that—my issue was that she had a boyfriend at home while she was doing this. My issue was about the morality of the situation—she was getting together with some guy two days after her boyfriend had visited her, and she was lying to him. I was like, "Girl, just be honest with him! Get it together!" But that all got distorted, and all of a sudden, I was the guy who hated interracial couples—which wasn't true.

The constant drama and distortion would retrigger me, over and over. If my sexuality came up, I'd have to talk about my father and how we had become estranged when he found out I was gay. Or there was an episode with a police officer, where I was in a white club with my white roommates, and the police surrounded me because they got an anonymous call that I had a gun.

I spent a lot of time curled up on that bench. From an outside perspective, it looked as though I was living the American dream—I was on this big TV show, right out of college. In reality, I was isolated and miserable. It was a chaotic atmosphere with no forward movement. It was an environment that bred conflict—and I could never get in front of it. Holding hands in a circle and singing "Kumbaya" doesn't get ratings.

With the cast of *The Real World: Philadelphia*. We were asked to pose in a way that "showed who we really were." I'm doing "power to the people" and a peace sign. Sums it up.

My family didn't even know I'd gotten the show until I was two months into filming. I didn't want them to crush my dreams. I thought if I told them I was going on *The Real World*, they were going to tell me no. They already didn't like that I was living in California. I was gay, I was rebellious, and the last thing I wanted to tell them was that I was going on an MTV reality show.

While we were filming, the producers gave us a free trip to Fiji. We were at a beautiful place eating dinner, and I wasn't even enjoying the moment. I was so upset and sick and hated everything about it.

Not that I wasn't thankful for *The Real World*. I am grateful that it gave me an opportunity to show my intelligence, and that it was a reflection for me to see myself from the outside. Truly, I wish everyone in their twenties could see their behavior recorded and played back to them, because I grew so much from that experience.

Despite my personal growth, however, the reality-show environment continually triggered me. At that dinner, one of the roommates asked, "What would we do if we were stuck on a deserted island, and it was just us?" Everyone started answering around the table.

"We would have parties all the time!"

"I would build us all huts!"

I was at the head of the table, and they finally got to me. Two of my roommates were dating—Landon and Shavonda. I joked that I would cut Landon's throat, because he was dating the only other black woman. I would procreate with her, so that we could make more children. And I would make all of them start working for me, and if they refused, I would stab them to death.

They were all like, "Dinner's ruined! Agh, I hate you, Karamo! You ruin everything!"

But I had to release some of the internal turmoil that I was experiencing. No one was giving me the space to work through my issues and figure them out, to be analytical and who I naturally am. My anxiety got channeled into deep, deep anger. It was my way of saying, "Don't fuck with me. I'm not in a good space." Obviously I would never stab anyone, but I wanted to paint an emotional picture for them that reflected the pain I was feeling. I was screaming out for help, but no one understood.

Now every time I hear a reality star say, "Oh, they edited me to look crazy," I say, "You're just not ready to own up to who you are. They can only edit what you say or what you do. If on Tuesday you call someone a bitch, and on Saturday you call someone else a bitch, it doesn't matter that it was edited together. You did it both times." Realizing that was a lesson for me. I learned that if I don't want to be edited a certain way, then I shouldn't act a certain way. I had to critically evaluate my actions and words in order to grow.

When I got off that show, I had instant notoriety, especially when I made an appearance on a college campus. I couldn't walk around people between the ages of thirteen to twenty-five without someone screaming, "Oh my God, it's Karamo from *The Real World*!" And I actually became Crazy Karamo. When I met my now-fiancé, Ian, one of his friends saw me looking at him before I first picked him up and started dating him. He whispered to Ian, "Girl, you don't want to date him. That's Crazy Karamo from *The Real World*."

It was rough, because after I got off the show, I felt like I had thrown away every single opportunity I had worked so hard for. I just ruined my life. I was traveling the world, making paid club appearances, but I was lost.

After the show, I couldn't go back to working in social services, because no one would hire me. I had to do the circuit of all the reality stars, doing the clubs and college-campus appearances and partying all night. Who was going to hire the kid who just acted the fool on reality television? Anytime I'd walk into an office, especially with the name Karamo, which is so memorable, they'd say, "Isn't that the guy from *The Real World*? We're not hiring him."

Also, I was the first openly gay black man on any reality show, ever. There had been another black man, from another season of *The Real World*, who everyone assumed was gay—and has since stated that he is. His name was Stephen, and everyone remembers that he slapped a girl who had Lyme disease. Because I was "crazy" and he was "crazy," and because we were both black, those stories started to intertwine. I'd walk into a place, and I'd hear, "Oh, not only is he crazy, he slapped a girl with a disease!"

In my mind, my life was ruined. For the first time, I didn't get to do what I normally did, which was to be mindful about my career and my path. Life became very hard—and the drugs, the depression, and the suicide attempt that followed didn't help.

I quit television altogether, and five years after *The Real World*, I moved back to Texas to be a father. I said to myself, *That's a wrap.*

That was an experiment; I'm glad I got it done in my twenties. Now that I'm in my thirties, I can bounce back.

I moved to Texas with my child (soon to be "children," after I adopted my second son, Christian, which you will also read about later) and started working for a health organization in a psychiatric ward. I worked in the juvie system as well, and really got back into what I had been trained to do. I was able to get a job, because by the time I had returned to Texas, I no longer had notoriety, except among college kids. There were so many reality shows coming out that by then, I was a footnote. And Kamilah knew someone at the organization, so she opened the door for me.

I just started excelling. It was my second shot at life—to finally do what everyone had told me to do. But in the back of my mind, something was still missing. I remember one day, my youngest son, Chris, who was eleven at the time, was sitting at the table and writing a paper on living your dream. He asked me in that moment if I was living my dream. It was the first time since I had been back in Texas, living this regular life, that I was faced with the question of what my dreams were.

Immediately the anxiety I felt as a child came back. Luckily, at that point, I was in a space where I knew how to read my body and my emotions. I knew how to recognize what was going on with me. I realized it wasn't anxiety I was feeling, but my system saying, *You're not living authentically and being who you are supposed to be. There's something that you're not finished with.*

That's what anxiety is. It's not necessarily that you're fearful. It can be something from your past, present, or future that you know you have to tackle.

In that moment, I was able to ask myself, *Where does this knot in my stomach come from?* In my mind, after going on *The Real World*, I stifled my dream of being an entertainer. But the knot in my stomach was telling me I didn't stifle it after all.

When Christian asked me if I was living my dreams, I knew in that moment I could either say, "Yes, I am," and tell him that working in social services was my dream, or be honest and say, "No, I'm not." I knew if I said no, I'd have to model the proper behavior. I didn't want to do to Chris what my father had done to me, which was to teach him to believe he couldn't go after his dreams.

I made a split-second decision as a parent and said, "No, son. I'm not living my dreams." With the innocence of a child, Chris asked, "Well, why aren't you?"

And I thought, *Well, because I have to provide for you, and you like to eat three meals a day.*

His question lingered with me as he was doing his homework. I went back to my room and started asking myself: *I'm twenty-nine, why am I not living my dreams?* I started to process every negative association with my dream that lived in my mind. I processed every moment on *The Real World* and why I "failed" at my dream the first time.

What I realized is: I didn't fail at my dream. My dream was to be like RuPaul, Phil Donahue, and Sally Jessy Raphael. *The Real World* was not that. The dream was to be on TV helping people.

I started to grapple with why I was afraid to tell my family that this was my dream.

Then I started calling everybody, and I did the exact opposite of what I had done before. I said, "This is my dream, and you all made me feel like that wasn't important. Why did you make me feel that way?" Sometimes it wasn't overtly expressed. There are a lot of unspoken truths in a family. Everything isn't a sit-down conversation. My expressing my dream was as simple as being at the dining room table and saying, "I think I want to try out for this play," and them saying, "You can't do that." Or my saying, "That looks like a cool job," and hearing them say, "It might be cool, but it's not real." People need to understand that they are always consciously or unconsciously affecting the choices and dreams of others.

I asked almost everyone in my family, "What about my dreams scared you?" All of them, one by one, said, "Because we didn't want you to fail. We wanted you to be happy." What I realized was that my dreams scared them because they were scared of their own dreams in a sense. They thought it was healthy to make me afraid of my dreams. Failure can be crippling, but to me, it's also a stepping-stone to greatness.

Right before I started community college in California to learn to become a host, I created this vision board. I was just looking at it, and I thought, *Oh my gosh, I have done a lot of that stuff already.*

Once I knew that, I started saying to myself, *I'm not afraid of my dreams. I am my dreams.* It was like clarity. I started writing down exactly what I wanted to do and created a vision board on a computer screen. I put a big picture of Oprah on there, holding her hands open. I put "LA home," because I had to get back to LA. I put "published author, *New York Times* bestseller."

I hung printouts of my mood board up everywhere, all over the house, specifically where the kids could see them. I wanted the message to be, "I'm not afraid of my dreams, and I don't want you to be afraid of your dreams."

I started thinking strategically about how I could get closer to those dreams. The first step was to get back into school. I started taking a community-college class in journalism in LA so I could learn how to be articulate on camera and read a prompter.

I was one of the oldest people in the class. It was full of all these young kids, and I was in the front row absorbing everything, taking notes, learning.

It was in that class that I found out from one of the students about an opportunity. A group of them was going out for an audition at the Oprah Winfrey Network—a brand-new network at the time, and they were looking for hosts. Even though I found out they were looking for one white male host and two female hosts of color—in other words, no one who looked like me—I decided I was still going to go for it. They didn't know I existed yet, so I wasn't going to settle.

Finding the courage to go after this opportunity was no easy task. After *The Real World*, my self-confidence wavered when it came to my career. I remember going to the bathroom before the audition, looking at myself in the mirror, and repeating, "You are not your past. You have prepared for your future. A yes can propel you, but a no will never hurt you." I kept saying that to myself, because I had to trick my mind into believing my dream was possible.

When I showed up at the audition, the woman who checked me in said, "We're not seeing men of color." She wasn't being prejudiced or anything—that's just not the demographic they were looking for.

I was like, "Please see me."

She said no.

Never being afraid of the word "no," I went back the next day, and she said no. I went back again a third time, and because I had been kind and sweet, she said, "Fine." In that audition, they asked me to talk about myself. I knew that this didn't mean I was supposed to ramble on and on. I talked about specific key points of my life, clearly and articulately, so that they could get a sense of who I am. All my training to be a good listener and talk about my emotions in high school and college came into play. All that work paid off.

Maybe two days later, I got a call telling me that I had made it to the next round of auditions for this Oprah Winfrey show called *The OWN Show*, for Oprah.com. I was ecstatic. I started running around the house, screaming, "Oh my gosh. This is it!"

In that next OWN audition, they said, "We see that there are some sexy photos of you out there." I had taken some sexy publicity shots after I had been on *The Real World*. I thought that was what I needed to do to get noticed and get work. Now I was mortified but I wanted to be clear about why they were out there. I had to tell them, "Yes, at one time, I did have sexy photos taken, because I didn't feel like I was worth it, after my experience of being on *The Real World*. I felt like I needed attention, and positive or negative attention was still attention. So if people were liking me because they wanted to sleep with me, or if my butt being out would get people to notice me, then why not? But I finally realized that I didn't need to be noticed that way. I don't judge anyone else who does, but I didn't. I became a father and began working on my self-esteem and self-love."

Eventually I got that job, and that job set me on the path to *Queer Eye*. Before I was on Netflix, I was working for Oprah Winfrey, the queen of talk, and being trained as a host with the people at her network.

If you look on Instagram, one of my first posts is the first bio that I ever had as a TV host, under OWN. When this bio came

My career was finally validated because I was working for OWN.

out, my family said, "This is a real job. We're so proud of you." My sons cheered me on, too. My name was right under Oprah Winfrey's name. When this website went live, it was the first time that my dreams were validated by my family.

When I initially arrived in LA, I had dreamed about being Oprah, but I thought my dream was too big. I couldn't be her. That was true: I could never be Oprah. But, I could be Karamo.

chapter **seven**

Fatherhood

Six months before I started ninth grade, my parents got a divorce. They had been growing apart for years, so the ending wasn't a shock. At that point, it was long overdue. The years of physical and emotional abuse my mother had gone through had finally come to an end. For the first time in my life, it was just the two of us: my mother and me. My sisters were in college, and Dad had decided to pick up and move to Florida to follow his dreams, whatever they were that week. We were on our own. It was a big change.

Mommy and I moved to the southwest side of Houston, which

was predominantly white and Asian at the time. I was zoned to Elsik High School, which was massive. I've been back there since, and it's not as big as I remembered it, but back then it felt like I was going to school in a stadium.

On the first day of school, I walked into the lobby to find several tables with the letters of the alphabet taped to the front of them. I looked for the table with "B," went up to the teacher attending the table, and received my locker combination, my schedule, and a map of the school. Lockers, schedule—it was the next phase of my life.

At that point, I was pretty clear on who I was as a young man. I'd already come to the point of identifying myself as gay. I'd already established myself as a good student. I was pretty secure.

I also had goals for my future. I kind of knew then that the best chance of escaping my life in Texas was to be a good high school student. To get out, I needed to go to a good college, and to do that, I needed good grades.

I walked to my locker, and the minute I got there, a young woman walked up to the locker next to mine. She was about five foot ten, had the biggest, most beautiful brown eyes I'd ever seen, and very full lips. She had on burgundy red lipstick, and her hair came to her shoulders.

I did not know a single person in this school. I turned to her and immediately said, "Hi, my name's Karamo. Would you like to be friends?"

She giggled, and when she did, I could see that she had a couple of crooked teeth on the bottom row of her mouth, which I thought was the sweetest thing ever. She tried to cover her smile, but I guess my candor about wanting to be friends made her smile so big that she couldn't hide it.

I thought, *This girl is sweet as pie*. There was nothing about me that was sexually attracted to her. I knew I was gay. Instead, I was like, *This is my first friend in this massive school. Already, my life is changing.*

Her name was Stephanie Brooks. We had been assigned lockers next to each other because our last names were close in the alphabet. We decided to walk to the auditorium together for freshman orientation. When we got in there, they again had us in alphabetical order, so we sat next to each other.

I couldn't tell you what the administrators said, because Stephanie and I were so busy giggling and talking about everything that came to mind. We talked about the girl sitting in front of us. We talked about the teacher making the announcements. We talked about her bus ride to school. I even started to open up about how my parents had recently gotten a divorce and how my mom and I had moved into an apartment complex not too far from school. She said, "Oh my gosh, I live in a similar apartment complex three minutes from there."

Stephanie told me that she lived with her grandma, because her mother was going through something, and that she didn't really have a relationship with her father. I mean, we got deep very quickly. The conversation continued when we realized we had our first two or three classes together.

Because we had met within the first fifteen minutes of school and had lockers next to each other, we just stayed friends. It was a fast friendship, to the point where it maybe took two weeks before we considered each other best friends. We walked home after school together every day. We rode the bus to school together. We ate lunch together. She was on the volleyball team, so I would stay after with her. I joined student government organizations, and she would stay after with me.

It was all very platonic. She was just someone I could relate to. As we were getting to know each other, we realized that we had both experienced a lot of trauma. We didn't have the words to say exactly that, because we were so young. But we knew that there was a lot of conflict in our families that plagued the both of us.

We connected through our shared interests and also through all the hard things we had experienced or had troubled feelings about. I felt safe around her, and she felt safe around me. Those conversations never were the focal point. When you're fifteen years old and trying to find the language to truly articulate the feelings you're having inside, it can be very difficult. What did come easy for us was an intrinsic sense that I was with someone who understood what I could not verbalize, and vice versa.

She would talk about her family members, and I would do the

same with mine. There were never any real follow-up questions or interjections or trying to one-up each other with the pain we felt. We were just being empathetic listeners. We both knew that we needed someone to talk to and express all the things that were going on in our minds. Neither of us had the life experience to truly give the other person advice on how to get through it.

We felt comforted in the fact that we were together. We wanted to be there for each other, as we were going through these issues in our lives that we didn't fully understand and didn't feel safe sharing with anyone else. Sometimes we would just hold hands quietly, in perfect understanding. As I reflect on our relationship, it was more mature in silence than many of the conversations I had with boyfriends as an adult.

Out of the two of us, I was the better student. I was always saying, "We have to get home, we have to do homework, we have to make sure we stay involved and not miss our club activities."

Stephanie was the one who was always like, "Let's not! Let's skip it!" It's funny, because I think now that if I had been straight, I would have probably followed her to skip school, because my hormones would have been like, "Do whatever the girl says so you can get something sexual."

Because I considered her my best friend, her persuasive ways didn't work on me! I said, "No, we're going to class. We're not skipping anything. We're doing homework." (When I talk to Stephanie, she jokes about that to this day.)

What did happen is that as we started getting closer, we had sort of an intimate moment where we decided to become boyfriend and girlfriend. I had told Stephanie I was gay, but I don't think she truly understood what that meant. Or maybe she didn't believe me or care.

Stephanie at fifteen, before we went to our first dance together. I bought her that stuffed animal you see in the background.

We were such close friends and we trusted each other. I think sharing my truth only made her feel even safer around me—like,

"Here's a young man who is not lying to me, who is not trying to hurt me and is also sharing something so intimate."

When I shared my sexual orientation with her, I immediately felt safe with her, too. I knew she wasn't going to run and tell her teammates. Yet people had these expectations that we should be dating because we spent so much time around each other. We both decided, "Let's just be boyfriend and girlfriend." We were continuing the same relationship—just with a different title.

After Christmas break, there was a shift. I could tell that even though I had told her I was gay, her emotions toward me had become a little bit deeper. There used to be an amusement park in Houston called Six Flags AstroWorld. One day, I went with three of my guy friends and made this tape in a karaoke booth where we sang the song "On Bended Knee," a now-classic Boyz II Men song that was popular on the radio back then.

The guys and I were horrible singers, so the tape was supposed to be comedic. I gave Stephanie a copy of the recording, because the other guys gave copies to their girlfriends. The message in that gesture was "Look, we're making a joke." But I remember her writing on the tape, "I love you so much, this is so sweet. Steph." With a heart.

She also wrote me a long letter, which said, "You're the love of my life, I love you, I'm so glad we're together."

I remember thinking, *Something's not right here*, but I was the only one thinking that. Stephanie had a different view of our relationship.

It made sense. She was a young girl, having nothing but the best time with this young man. She was straight. We were very loving. Of course she was going to develop feelings.

One day, we decided to skip school. I was actually behind on a project, because I had exhausted myself with all the stuff I was doing in school. In my mind I justified skipping by saying, "If I take a sick day, I can get the project done." My mother worked during the day and would not be home. I suggested we skip school together—which Stephanie loved. But I could sense that in her mind, I was asking her to skip school with me as more than just friends.

That day, we walked to the bus together and then came back to the house after I knew my mother had left for work. At this point, my mom was working as a dental assistant at a private office on the opposite side of town, and she wouldn't be home until around 6:00 p.m. I opened the door and Stephanie walked in, looking particularly beautiful. I could tell she had taken extra care with her appearance.

We sat in my living room. I started working on my project, and she turned on the TV. It was ten thirty in the morning. The phone rang, and I picked it up! I was supposed to be at school; why in the hell did I pick up the phone? It was just a natural impulse. I said hello and heard my father's voice, calling from Florida to speak to my mother. I knew I was in trouble and started freaking out internally.

My father asked me what I was doing at home. Stephanie tried to whisper something in the background, helping me figure out what to say, and my father heard her. He exclaimed, "You have a girl over there?"

I hesitated, and finally said, "Yes, sir."

He laughed. "All right," he said. "Have a good time, son." Then he hung up. I stared at the phone in stunned silence. I wasn't in trouble for skipping school or having a girl in the house. It was like I was in some weird twilight zone.

I finished the project before noon, and then Stephanie said, "We should start making out." As a young man of fifteen who had never kissed anybody at that point, I had a natural curiosity about making out. (I wish I could be like, *Yeah, I was a playa!* But, I wasn't.)

So I shyly replied, "Okay, let's try it."

We started making out, which was nice. It wasn't that first awkward teen kiss you hear about—it went smooth, and it felt good. And then, next thing you know, she took off my shirt, and I took off her shirt. She took off my shorts, and I took off her pants. The entire time, I was thinking, *I don't know if I want to be doing this. This doesn't feel right to me.*

My mind was saying, *You really don't want this,* but my fifteen-year-old body was saying, *This is the first time someone is touching you? We're gonna react.*

Stephanie said she was a virgin and asked in that moment if I was, too.

"Of course I am," I said.

She smiled. "Do you want to lose our virginity to each other?" she asked. Very matter-of-fact, but still intimate and safe.

I said, "Sure."

We went into my bedroom and tried for about ten minutes— clearly, I had no idea what to do.

Any pornography I had watched up until that point was just with two men. In my mind, I knew what to do with a man in a room, but I didn't know what to do with a woman. So we kind of tussled around. In the pornography with men I had watched, as it progressed, they sort of got more aggressive. But I was handling a young woman, and I didn't know how it progressed with a woman. So it was just very awkward.

I knew it wasn't working, but my body still wanted to go for it. Which was the message Stephanie was focusing on. We decided to stop, and then she said, "Let's go into the bathroom. I'm going to take a shower." She asked if I wanted to take one with her. We got in the shower together, and within two minutes, we lost our virginities to each other. She sort of took the lead on what to do, and where things went, for lack of a better phrase.

My first time lasted a total of two and a half minutes. Then I hopped out of the shower very awkwardly, because I had never experienced an orgasm with another person. I was frightened, and I left her there.

I ran to my room, thinking, *What just happened? What the hell is going on?* At this point, my body had caught up with my mind, and it was like, *Nope! Never again! Not doing this!*

Stephanie eventually came out of the shower and joined me in the room. As I think back on it now, I feel horrible. Her first experience was with somebody who was so inexperienced and who was also dealing with the conflict of his sexuality. I can't imagine what it was like for her to have to watch me run out of the shower like that. No cuddling or kissing. No sharing of an intimate moment after her first time. I lost my virginity a second time, when I first engaged in a sexual experience with a man. I was older then and able to control the situation, but she didn't get a do-over like I did. I know we were both kids, but I still wish I had made that moment special for her.

We stayed best friends after that. We continued to talk, and nothing changed, except for the fact that there was never gonna be any more sex. It was clear as day for me. Though she never brought it up and never pressured me, I think it did finally click for her: *Oh, he* is *gay.* We still felt safe with each other and loved and supported each other. That experience happened in February, but then, a few months later, she and her family moved.

I didn't even get to tell her goodbye, because on the last day of school, my mother came into my bedroom, and said, "Your father and I talked, and we decided you're going to spend tenth grade in

Florida and live with him for the rest of your high school experience. In the next two days, you're getting on a plane, and you're moving." What the hell? You're telling me I have to uproot myself and go make new friends? I was completely broken up about it. Despite that, I was not going to disrespect them, nor was I going to pout. It just wasn't in my personality.

I understood why. Even at that time, my mother was going through her own phase of growth and healing. She found out that I had skipped school and had done a couple of other rebellious things. I was far from perfect—I did act out sometimes. There was a time during Christmas that Stephanie and I stole some clothing from a department store. We stole clothes because I wanted to get everyone Christmas gifts, but I didn't have a job. We didn't get caught at the store, but my mother caught me when she found the bag of stolen items.

I think she could sense that if I wasn't put in check quickly, I might mess up my future—although my grades had never dropped. I think she thought I was acting out because I was missing my dad. The solution was to get me to him.

They made that decision without consulting me, and I had no choice but to do what they decided. Two days after ninth grade was done, I was on a plane to Florida, to live with my father, in Parkland. The only thing I felt sad about was that I didn't get a chance to call Stephanie and say goodbye. This was before everyone had cell phones and social media, when you can stay in contact with anyone no matter where they are. Once I moved, I didn't know how to reach her, and she didn't know how to reach me.

I moved to Florida with my dad. On my first day of school, I met my best friend Ray. I had an amazing high school experience at Marjory Stoneman Douglas, which later became notorious because of the horrific school shooting (which is part of the reason why I'm so passionate about the issue of gun legislation reform and adequate mental health support for youth).

I went on to Florida A&M and met my second best friend, Tre. I had an amazing experience there and then moved to California and got on *The Real World*. Time went on. To be honest, I never thought of Stephanie again.

One Friday night in California, I came home from an MTV *Real World* event, hungover. I was using drugs excessively at this point, and my mental health was deteriorating. I was going through a conflict with my boyfriend. My relationship with my father had dissolved. The last thing I was thinking about was anybody from ninth grade.

As I walked toward my apartment door in a sort of stupor, because I was depressed and coming down from the drugs I had just done, I noticed a stack of papers on my welcome mat. I stumbled over to them, opened the envelope, and all I saw on the front page was "Texas Attorney General's Office." I quickly looked at the second page, and it read, "Subpoena for Back Child Support."

Immediately, I thought, *Ashton Kutcher is inside my house. I'm getting punked! Punk'd* was a popular MTV show that aired in the 2000s that played practical jokes on actors, musicians, and reality stars. I was honestly thinking, *What's funnier than punking the twenty-five-year-old gay guy and making him think he has a baby?*

I got so excited. I was about to meet Ashton Kutcher! Ashton is so sexy! I couldn't believe they were finally doing a *Real World* episode of *Punk'd*! I ran down to my car, which had some luggage in it. I changed into something nice (gotta look cute!). Then I picked up the paperwork and opened the door slowly.

I lived with Ray, but he wasn't home. I was thinking, *There's usually someone there to get the story going, like an accomplice. Ray must be here waiting for me.* So I turned on the lights and said, "Hey, Ray! I'm home! I'm here!" We lived in a very spacious two-bedroom, two-bath, with a big living room and two balconies. But no one was in the house. I went to the balcony. No one was there.

So then I thought, *Maybe this paperwork is for someone else.* In my aggravation, I threw the papers on my dining room table. I didn't think about them again. I went into my bedroom, took a shower, and went to bed.

At around two thirty in the morning I woke up and got some juice to drink. I sat down at my dining room table and started looking at the paperwork. Then I saw, on the third page in bold black letters: "Stephanie Brooks." I literally spit out the juice I was drinking. That was the first time since ninth grade I had seen her name.

I looked underneath her name, and I saw "Karamo Brown." What the hell?

Under that was the phrase "Order of Paternity," and under that, I saw a third name: "Jason Rashad Brown." I started shaking. I thought, *Okay, if this is a joke, this is a really well-researched joke. No one knows about the girl I lost my virginity to. No one knows this stuff. Whoever did this did way too much research, and it's not funny.*

I saw that Jason's birthday was in 1996. No, it couldn't be. But if I did the math, that would have been about the time. I saw that Stephanie had four other children, because they were listed on there. I saw Houston, Texas. Then I saw an alarmingly large number for back child support: $230,000, along with a notice informing me that I had a few weeks to pay the fee, or they would start garnishing my paychecks and put liens on my personal property.

Fear coursed through my body, and now I was fully freaking out. I started pacing around the room, processing. *Do I have a kid? I don't know where Ray is. Who can I call?* Part of me still thought it was a sick joke, but I knew in my heart that it was no joke. I just kept thinking, *How? How? How?*

The next morning came, and I called my mother and my sisters. They had the same reaction: This is a joke. There's no possible way. Ray came home from his girlfriend's house, and he couldn't believe it, either. Everyone was in a state of shock.

But no one was in a bigger state of shock than me. My mind

was just buzzing with thoughts like, *What have I done? What is going on with this child? What is going on with Stephanie? How many people have I hurt? My life is finished.*

My mother just said calmly, "You need to wait until Monday morning, and then you need to make a call to the Texas attorney general's office so you can get more information." I spent the entire weekend in the house. Luckily Ray and Tre were there, and they were very much in the space of, "You're not going out; you're not going to go find drugs. You're gonna stay in this house and calm yourself down. We're going to wait until Monday, and then we're gonna figure this out."

So I stayed in the house. I remember going on MySpace, which I hadn't been on in a while. I had been on *The Real World*, so I had tons of messages that I hadn't gone through. I scanned through the messages and I saw one from a woman named Stacy. I opened the message and it read, "Karamo, this is Stephanie's sister. You know you've got a kid. Do the right thing, and come step up for your kid."

I literally backed away from the screen, thinking, *What the hell is going on? This is way too much. I'm getting paperwork from the courts; Stephanie's sister is coming out of the woodwork contacting me. I'm not equipped to deal with this.* I didn't respond to the message. I just closed the screen and thought, *I'm done with all y'all.*

Monday came, and I called the number on the paperwork and I gave them the case number. The woman on the phone said, "Sir, unfortunately, I can't give you any information on the phone, because paternity is not confirmed. I don't know if you're actually the father. You have to come in person to get the information you're requesting."

I called my mother and sisters to share what I was told by the clerk at the attorney general's office. Within two hours, I had a plane ticket to Houston, leaving the next day. The night before I left, I decided I was going to have one more bender before I stepped into the pending shit-show awaiting me in Houston.

I went out; I partied; I did a bunch of coke. And as I mentioned in chapter 5, that's when I emptied my pockets like normal into the tray at the airport without thinking and I realized that there was a leftover bag of cocaine going through the security X-ray machine.

The bag made it through, and I finished it in the bathroom. I was already flying high when I got on the plane. Once in the air I fell asleep pretty quickly—and I had nightmares of a twelve-foot angry child who was trying to beat me up. I woke up in a cold sweat, thinking, *What the fuck?*

I got to Houston, and my sister picked me up. She could tell that I was still high. She said, "Nope, you're not doing this. You have a future; you have a child who is potentially going to need you; you have to get your shit together." I stayed in her house for four weeks, under her supervision. She was getting me mentally prepared and back on track before the paternity test.

Finally, I felt a little bit healthier, and she felt better about it.

After three weeks, I went to the Texas attorney general's office to complete the paternity test. They said it would take two weeks. Once the results came back, they'd give me the information that I wanted, whether the child was indeed mine. It was legal in 1996 to name a father on a birth certificate without his being present and without paternity being confirmed. So I was named the father, even though I wasn't sure if he was actually mine.

Two more weeks flew by. I tried to look up Stephanie on social media, and I couldn't find her anywhere. I kept thinking, *They could be right here in town, in Houston, and I wouldn't even know.* Sometimes I would take my sister's car and drive around our old neighborhood, thinking I might see her if she still lived in that area, and maybe I'd see my potential child, too.

I started having all these delusions—like if we were in a restaurant, I would think, *That boy next to me could be my child.* I had no idea what he looked like; every child I saw could have been mine. I was also wrestling with the fact that this might not even be my child. There was still the chance I could go back to LA and all this would have been a bad dream.

I never once thought fatherhood was something I was going to engage in. I was so young, and still dealing with problems of my own. Parenting was not something that was happening for me—at least, not for a long time.

Then we got the call on my sister's house phone: I needed to come in to the attorney general's office. I got there and I waited in line. They called me up to the window. The woman said, "You're the father. All the information you need is in the packet. *Next!*"

I said, "Excuse me, ma'am, I have some questions, I have—"

The more questions I asked, the more aggravated she got. "Everything you need is in the packet, sir," she said loudly. "Next."

I went back to the car and opened the packet. It said the chances of my being the father were 99.99999 percent. It had Stephanie's information at the top of the sheet—no phone number, only an address. So I did what any sane adult would do: I drove to that address, unannounced. It was now or never.

It was about one o'clock in the afternoon. I knocked on her door. A little girl opened the door, and I asked if Stephanie was home. "Mom!" she yelled. Around the corner walked Stephanie Brooks. Immediately she saw my face, and I saw hers. She started crying, and we started hugging.

In that moment, all the feelings of anger and confusion went away. I was looking at my best friend again. It was like we were transported back to being fifteen, when we were excited to see each other. She invited me in, we sat down, and she told me the story. She said that after her mother found out that she was pregnant, she made her move away. She didn't know how to get in touch with me. She was scared that I had already found a better life, and she didn't want to ruin it.

She was sixteen and raising a kid—not that her life was ruined, but it was harder. She didn't want to do that to me. As time passed, she got too scared to bring it up. Later, she had her other kids, all from the same man—but that relationship had since ended.

I asked her how the courts had found me. She said she applied for state welfare benefits and had listed me as the father on Jason's birth certificate. The state had found the father without telling her. She had no idea that the state had contacted me and no idea that I was showing up at her house. It was a complete shock to her.

In that moment, it reaffirmed the feeling I first had when I saw her—this was my best friend. She wasn't contacting me out of the blue to be malicious or spiteful. She wasn't coming after me for my money. Everybody was making her out to be the villain, but she wasn't. She didn't know they were contacting me. She was just a young girl coming from a broken home and doing the best she could, who applied for benefits to support her children. All she wanted was a little assistance, to make sure her kids were fed and clothed and living a happy life. Some clerk took it upon himself to find me.

I apologized. She apologized, and we started talking. We didn't talk about my son, or her other kids. We talked about fashion, music—all the stuff we talked about as teens. Once we forgave each other, it was like we were fifteen again, in front of our lockers.

I always felt the need to be an open book with her. Then, one of her kids walked through the door, and she said, "Oh my gosh— Jason will be home soon." I thought, *Oh, right, I'm a father! What the fuck?*

She asked if I wanted to meet him, and I said, "Of course." She told me to give her some time to prepare him, and that I should come back later. So I went back to my sister's house and told her I was going back that night to meet Jason. My sister was relieved to find out that Stephanie was a good person and didn't have some secret agenda for contacting me.

I needed to figure out something for Jason and me to do, so I planned to take him bowling. In every sitcom I'd ever seen, the dad goes bowling with his child when they need to connect and have a hard conversation. That's what you do: go bowling and have heart-to-hearts over a soda. I thought that if we went bowling, we'd have an activity to distract us but still get to be together privately.

I got to Stephanie's house around seven o'clock. I was anxious; my hands were sweating. As I sat in the car, a little voice in my head was saying, *Karamo, you don't have to do this. You're a child, and you're supposed to go in there and raise a child? You don't even have a relationship with your father at this point, so you don't even have a man who you can talk to about this. Run for your life.*

My sisters were career-focused and didn't have any kids, and neither did my best friends. There was no one I could talk to about what I was feeling. All the fears and doubts I had about ruining my child's life began playing like a broken record in my head. I thought, *No one's going to blame you if you just turn around, drive away, and go back to California. Just go. Send the check. When he turns eighteen he'll find you. Deal with it then.*

At the same time, I thought, *What if he needs me? What if there's a reason for this? I must find the courage to face this.* So I got out of the car, walked slowly to Stephanie's front door for the second time that day, and knocked—unsure of who was going to greet me or how my life was going to change once this door opened. The door opened, and it was Stephanie. I sighed with relief.

To this day, when I see Stephanie, I just feel love. There's never a place in my heart where I feel anything bad about her. I know she feels the same about me. Our relationship is as strong now as when we were fifteen. I think it's because our relationship started on such a pure and positive note that nothing could break it.

Stephanie invited me in. Her family was there; the sister who messaged me was there. Stephanie's two other daughters were sitting on the couch. Stephanie's new boyfriend was also there, staring at me like he wanted to beat me up. (I'm thinking, *Guy, I'm gay. I don't want anything to do with your girlfriend. But I get it.*) At that point, I was feeling the pressure.

She lived in a tiny two-bedroom apartment. Earlier in the day, I hadn't looked around or noticed the space. With the place full of people, it occurred to me that Stephanie, five kids, and her boyfriend were all living in this really small two-bedroom space.

On the other hand, I lived in a massive two-bedroom in LA. Just being in her apartment made me feel claustrophobic—I couldn't imagine how she maintained it with all those people living there. But everyone was happy, and no one seemed sad or depressed. Immediately, putting the pieces together, I realized that she had to be a great mother. They were in this small apartment, but everyone looked happy. Nobody was crying or snot-nosed. The kids were looking lovely. The boyfriend looked nice. It was clear to me that she was providing as best she could.

Then she called, "Jason! Come out here! Your dad's here." It was the first time I had heard someone refer to me as a dad. Around a corner ran this little boy, who grabbed my left leg and held on to it. And at this point, I had no idea what Jason looked like, because I'd never seen a picture. I looked at Stephanie, wide-eyed, with a forced smile, because I was excited but nervous. I asked if the boy was Jason, and she said, "No, that's Christian." It was her other son.

While Christian was on my leg, Jason slowly walked around the corner. He was very shy—it was written all over his face and in his body language. There's something about the first moment of seeing your child. Even though I had anxiety, all the pieces of me that I felt were missing just got sewn up. It was like I could feel them getting sewn up internally the minute I saw his face.

I fell in love with him immediately, and we had just met. All the heartbreak I had experienced, all the sadness—just looking into his sweet eyes made me feel that I had a purpose. I started feeling so good about life. I looked at him, this little fourth-grade boy, as he was slowly walking toward me. I thought, *This is my chance to do everything right again. I can do this. I can do this.*

He walked up to me, put his hand up shyly as if to shake mine, and said, "Hi, I'm Jason." Trying to break the ice, I replied, "No hand-shaking. Come give your dad a hug." I grabbed him and gave him the biggest hug I could. I just held on to him so tightly. In hindsight, I now know that I was really holding on to the little boy inside of me, hugging him.

Neither of us was alone. We had each other.

Stephanie asked us if we wanted to take a photo, and she snapped one. My first photo as a father is with Jason on my right side, and with Christian, crouched down on the floor, still holding on to my left leg.

The irony of it all is that now, having full custody of both of them, at the ages of twenty-one and eighteen, it's like I met both of my sons the first day I ever walked into that house—and didn't know it. It's kind of crazy, because none of Stephanie's other kids ran up to me that day. There was something in Christian that made him go, "You're my dad, too!" I'll get back to that.

I asked Jason if he wanted to go bowling, and he said yes. We went to a bowling alley near Stephanie's apartment that I quickly realized was near Rice University. When I walked in, everybody freaked out, because Karamo from *The Real World* had just come in.

The night I took Jason bowling to get to know him better.

Everyone started yelling, "Oh my gosh, Karamo! What are you doing here?" I told them I was there with my son, and they all yelled, "What the fuck are you talking about? You're gay; you don't have a son! Come drink with us!"

Up until this point, having fun with college kids was a large part of my identity. It was how I was making a living—partying with the college kids, doing appearances at clubs. I remember, distinctly, starting to get sucked into it, because I didn't have the language to say, "Back off, I'm with my son."

Then the catalyst for me to find that language finally came. A young girl wanted to get me in a photo. She was being very aggressive, and she pushed Jason in order to get to me. Suddenly, my fatherly instincts took over and I was like, *Get the fuck away from Jason.* "Do *not* push my kid," I told her loudly. It startled everyone.

As I pushed my way out of the crowd to reach Jason, I could hear them saying, "He is crazy," and "Fuck him; he's a nobody anyway." They were speaking at a volume that not only I could hear but that Jason could hear, too.

They were cussing at me and telling me to calm down. I decided the best thing to do was to remove myself and take Jason to the other side of the bowling alley. I got a booth at the very far end—although I could still hear the people cackling, because they had just met Crazy Karamo. But I was determined that no matter what, I needed to connect with my son, even though he was very shy and didn't really know what to say.

Then he said, "I've seen you before." I asked him what he meant and he said, "I know why those people are acting that way. The first time I saw you, my aunt Stacy said, 'There's your dad on TV.' And you were in a shower with another guy."

I started freaking out. The first time my child saw me, I was in the shower with another man on MTV's *The Real World*. Oh man. This was not going to be as easy as I thought.

I quickly changed the subject and said, "Let's bowl." So for the next thirty minutes, we probably said four words to each other. I didn't know what to say, and he didn't know what to say. We did have some laughs as I realized that we were both horrible bowlers. (I thought, *Here's the first genetic connection.*) We ate some pizza. Then I looked at the clock, saw it was 9:00 p.m., and told him I had to get him home.

As we got to the house, I asked him if he was ready for school the next day. This is the moment that I really became the father I am today. Jason said, "No, I'm not really prepared for tomorrow, I didn't do my homework." I said, "What? You were out bowling and eating snacks, and you didn't do your homework? That is not acceptable! You're going in the house right now, I'm coming in with you, and you're not going to sleep until you do your homework!"

I walked inside as if I owned the house and was like, "Get to this table: you're doing your homework." He did it that night with me watching. He laughs with me about it now, because as I mentioned, in my family homework and education were big things. But Jason's mother had a very relaxed attitude when it came to schoolwork. When she found out she was pregnant, she had to drop out of high school. She was only able to get her GED, so schoolwork had not been part of her life for a while.

Once he was finished, I tucked him in. I went home and just sat in bed, replaying the fact that I had just hugged my son. The next day, I went into full daddy mode. I quickly rearranged my schedule so that I could take Jason to school in the morning and pick him up in the afternoon. I wanted to be there for him after all the years that I had missed. When I got there and realized he wasn't doing the best in school, I did what my parents did for me and started figuring out a plan. I got super involved and met with the principal and all of Jason's teachers. I began volunteering so that I could be at the school while he was there. The phrase "helicopter dad" doesn't do justice to my behavior. I was even more intense. It was because I needed to get him on the right track, and I knew I couldn't do that by being a part-time dad.

Stephanie, being supportive, was like, "Yes, go for it!" I found out that Jason had failed a grade, so I talked to the counselor and asked what we needed to do to get him back in the right grade. We formulated a plan. It was like I started doing everything that my parents had done to give me my best life. I wanted the same thing for Jason: I wanted to make life better for him.

Jason, Nedra, and Kamilah. This was when I was first getting to know my son, and it was important that he got to know my sisters, too. We all went everywhere together. We took him to museums, art shows—and this was at *The Nutcracker*, his first play ever.

Immediately, you could see a change in him, because his style went from baggy clothes to things like tight, skinny purple jeans—skater style. Although he wanted to be a skater and liked those kinds of clothes, his family members on his mom's side had told him that was too "gay." Black men didn't act that way.

And I said, "Nope! People did that to me, and that was not okay. So, Jason, when you come with Dad, you can wear anything you want! You can be a skater." Our relationship started to grow quickly, because he enjoyed the structure and discipline, but Dad also loved him for him. I would tell him, "If you do something wrong, or there's something you want to be, and you tell me the truth, you'll never get in trouble. But if you don't tell me the truth and lie to me, then you'll be in trouble."

The reason I did this is because when I was a kid, I used to think how backward it was that when I did something wrong and admitted it, I got in trouble. Honesty should never be punished. It should be celebrated, because it gives your child a chance to grow—even if they're being honest about doing the wrong thing.

Because of that attitude, to this day, Jason and I have a 100 percent honest relationship. He can tell me anything. If he gets himself into trouble and tells me the truth about what he's done, he doesn't get punished by me. But if I find out he doesn't tell me, he's in trouble. Or if he has a dream, and has hidden it from me because he's scared that I'm going to discourage him, we have something to talk about.

If he has a dream and he goes after it, I'm going to support him. I'm going to give him advice and help navigate it so he doesn't make any bad decisions. I'm never going to make him feel bad for his truth.

Right before Jason started a program to get back into his right grade at the end of his fifth-grade year (he eventually skipped seventh grade and went straight to eighth), I went to his mother. I told her that he was doing really well and flourishing around me. I said, "You have all these other kids. I want to take custody of him to give him more opportunities and help support you."

In the sweetest voice, she said, "Thank you. I will agree to this if you promise me one thing: that you'll keep us as a family."

I said immediately, "I can promise you that."

To this day, Stephanie has been invited to every big event in my life, even though she isn't in the same state as me. She's been involved in everything. She was even at my engagement party. It was important to me that the mother of my children be there as I said, "Please marry me" to the man I love. She's my family, and our family has to stay tight.

In the meantime, after I took that paternity test and found out I was a father, I put in a dispute with the state. This would buy me more time so that my lawyer could put together a case about the back child support. However, when Stephanie and I decided that I would take full custody of Jason, this ended the case—to the surprise of both of us.

Me with Jason. You can see I wanted to be cool, with my backward base-
ball cap and my cell phone with the earpiece. But I was also in full dad
mode. Like, the shirt I'm wearing says, DRUGS ARE WIGGITY WACK—I mean,
how "dad" is that?

Two months after I talked to Stephanie about getting full custody, Jason moved in with me. He was happy and expressed that to
me often. Even though I was more disciplined when it came to
schoolwork, he was having a blast. "I feel like an only child," he
would say happily—because all the attention was on him, all the
gifts were for him, and he had a room all to himself.

As for me, I decided to stay in Texas because I was doing so
well with being sober. I was getting clarity on my own dreams. Just
being around Jason made me a better man. People always say that I
saved his life, but he saved my life.

The kids and me driving around. I'm being an annoying selfie dad.

Jason made me whole again. He made me realize there was a purpose to my life. He made me realize I could dream again, and I didn't have to be afraid. Even as I was raising him, he was raising me to be a good dad. I decided that part of my promise to Stephanie to keep our family together was to stay in Texas for the next year and a half to two years before I brought him to California to live with me.

During that time, I got a job back in social services. I was working; life was great. One day I got a call from Stephanie that there was a family emergency that concerned Christian. Christian and Jason were very close, so whenever Jason and I had activities, Christian always came along. Every time we took a road trip, Christian went, too. He was always with us. He was also the only one of Stephanie's other kids who had met every single member of my family.

This is a moment from Christian's birthday, after I got some frosting on his nose. I think he was 11.

When I found out about this emergency, I sprang into action. Chris was in a detention program. We found out there was an issue going on with Chris that I'm not going to go into, because it's his story to tell. Due to this conflict, they were planning to remove Christian from Stephanie's home and temporarily place him in the custody of the courts. Because I worked in social services, I said, "Well, he can come and stay with me. I'm an approved home."

I didn't want to separate the family, and I didn't want him in foster care. Stephanie was a great mom, and this situation had nothing to do with her, yet the entire family was being punished. I thought, *Let's figure it out while he's with me, where he feels safe.* So he moved in with me, which was supposed to be temporary. When he did that, it was like a light bulb went off in his head. With the

With the kids at a family gathering. Jason is taller than me now and Chris is my height. When did I become the short one?

discipline and the love he was getting from me, everything just started working.

After six months, Christian was doing so well. One Saturday morning, I was in bed and he came and knocked on my bedroom door. At this point, he was accustomed to Jason calling me Dad while he called me Uncle Karamo. This time, he walked in the room and said, "Hey, Dad, can I go outside and skate a little bit?"

I was like, *Oh my gosh, I have* two *kids.* He had organically just called me Dad. It didn't shock me the same way it did when Stephanie said, "Jason . . . your dad's here." It felt natural. It felt good. I said simply, "Yes, Son. You can go outside." He went outside, and I called Stephanie and said, "Christian's doing really well. How about I become his legal guardian, just to get him well and back on the right path?"

Once again, she said, "I love you. Will you keep our family together?"

I said yes. Christian came back upstairs, and I said, "Your mother and I talked. Would you like to live here permanently with me?"

He said yes and jumped into my arms. He and Jason high-fived.

When I called my mother and told her the news, she said, "I always knew that would happen. We all knew. We all saw that you had two sons. You just didn't know."

To be clear, it was very hard and stressful taking on two kids. Time management became an issue, because I was focusing on their needs while still trying to pursue mine. I also had to take

Christian to therapy twice a week for several years. Sometimes I felt like I was drowning, but I just kept asking for support from those I love and kept being honest about how I was feeling. Many parents feel guilty or sad for admitting they can't do it all, but I let that toxic way of thinking go. I was aware that I needed help if success was going to be an option.

After I became Christian's guardian, he really started flourishing. Eight months after moving in with me, I decided to bring him and Jason to California. The kids were so excited. We got in a U-Haul truck and drove to California on I-10, just like I did after college—only this time, I was a father of two boys.

The kids in the U-Haul, ready to get on the 10 Freeway to head to California with me.

Now they're happy and healthy. We've had plenty of growing pains, but we're a strong family unit. I treat them like young adults, and I'm helping guide their lives. That's my journey in fatherhood.

Keeping the family tight: Me, Christian, Stephanie, and Jason. June 2018. All together and very happy.

The funny thing is that I'm my father's only boy. One issue he had when he found out I was gay is that the family name would end with me. I was the last Brown, and when my sisters got married they would take different names.

Ironically, the name didn't end with me. However, one of my goals with Jason was to break our "family curse" of being a parent by the age of sixteen. For the past four generations, every male in my family has had a child by the age of sixteen. I was the fourth generation, and when I began identifying as gay, they thought that I would break that curse. But I didn't.

When I got Jason, it became my mission to make sure the family curse was broken. I did that by doing something that was the opposite of my father.

Instead of talking about sex without the context of love and intimacy, I discussed sex with Jason in a way so he could understand that it should be special, a shared intimacy. But more so, I realized that all the language that schools and parents use with children is to tell them to abstain. I switched it to, "I know you have desires, but I would like you to wait." I wasn't laying down the law. I was telling him what I would like to happen.

I realized that no one ever said to me, "I would like you to wait." I said to him, "If you want to engage in an intimate moment with a young woman, I'd like you to wait. I promise you, it's so much better when you're older, when you can understand it and you're emotionally equipped."

I'm proud to report that Jason didn't lose his virginity until he was twenty years old to a girl he loved. Generational curse broken!

Fatherhood has taught me how to be a better man and human being. You see your actions, hopes, and fears reflected back at you daily through your children's eyes. It makes you want to work a little harder each day to be a better person for them—and to create the best world possible for them to live in.

chapter eight

Hopes for the Future

Family is important to me and something I've always wanted. Since I was a child, I've wanted to get married and have a husband. (Kids were something I never really considered, but luckily, the Lord blessed me with children.)

Now that Jason and Christian are getting older, I'm realizing that grandkids could be an option one day! Which is so crazy to me. I hope it's in another ten years, but I'm also aware that it could happen at any point.

Marriage has always been important to me, especially after seeing my own parents' marriage fall apart. I've always wanted to get married and have a family like the Huxtables on TV (the characters, not Bill Cosby).

I'd also always told myself that when I got the kids I would not introduce them to a man unless that man was the one I was going to spend the rest of my life with.

I remember the day I walked out of a club in California and Ian walked by. For a few years, we went to the same clubs and I would see him sporadically when I was out, but there was never any communication. Actually, I'd had a crush on him back then—but I was in a relationship, so Ian was off-limits.

Ironically, Ian was the one person who made my then-boyfriend jealous. He could see it in my eyes that when I saw Ian walking by, there was something there. I think I sort of crafted the idea of Ian being my future husband way before we actually got together.

My birthday is in November (I'm a Scorpio). When I was twenty-nine and about to turn thirty, I decided to have a birthday party. I rented a big house in Malibu. It was more than a birthday party—it was a celebration of the fact that I was now sober, the kids were doing great, my family relationships were getting stronger, and I was back working in social services and helping people.

All my friends and family were going to come. I was still living in Houston with the kids but I had a clear plan of how to get them back to LA after they finished school in Houston that June. Then I was going to start pursuing my career as a television host.

The night before the party, I went to a club. As I was walking out, Ian walked by. Now, I had not seen Ian in maybe five years—but when I saw him that night, it was like a ghost ran through me. I got chills up and down my entire body.

I started to feel this sort of anxiety in the pit of my stomach, which told me, *You can't let him walk away. There's no option.* Being someone who knows how to make a split-second decision, I turned around. Ian was maybe forty paces up the street with one of his closest friends, a guy named William, and I sprinted toward him.

His back was to me. Once I got to him, I flipped him around and picked him up. He had no idea what was going on, because some crazy stranger had literally picked him up at about one in the morning. So he started hitting my head, and saying, "Put me down!"

As I did I said, "Hi, Ian. Karamo." He looked at me and then started smiling, as if he was excited to see me. As if he was seeing an old friend. We just stood on the side of Santa Monica Boulevard in West Hollywood and we stared at each other, smiling, for what seemed like ten minutes.

I told him I was having a birthday party the following night in Malibu and invited him to come. I said, "All of my family will be there, and I'd really like for you be there, too." He said okay. We opened up our Razr flip phones—this was a few years ago, okay?—and exchanged telephone numbers.

I didn't even want to go back to the club at that point. I went home and my mom, Kamilah, and Nedra were staying at my house and were still awake. I stood in front of them. "Everybody," I announced, "the man I am spending the rest of my life with is coming to the party tomorrow night." They looked at me like I was crazy, but I knew it. I just knew it.

The next morning, I was the first one up and I was so excited. This guy I'd had a crush on for years was coming to my party. I was so joyful getting ready, because I was peacocking for him as well— *Look at how my life has gotten better! I'm looking good! Meet my family!*

As I've mentioned, family is important to me—if I'm going to have a guy meet my family on our first get-together, that's major.

The party starts that night. The first hour passes. The second hour passes. The third hour passes. The fourth hour passes. And there is no Ian. He doesn't show. The party ends, and I am devastated and embarrassed, because I had told everybody, over and over again, that he was coming.

The next morning, I woke up and thought, *This is not fair. I'm not going to let this pass.* Everyone around me said, "Let it go. Forget it. Whatever. You're going back to Texas after this, and maybe when you move back out to LA in the summer, you'll see him."

I thought, *No. We are adults. It is not okay to ghost on somebody. Just communicate, "I didn't want to come." It's fine. Communication is okay!*

At that point in my life, I wasn't accepting anything less than communication. I knew that communication was hard for some people, but I also knew that it could work if you gave them the opportunity, if you just opened the door. I wanted to open that door for Ian.

So I de-escalated my tone and gave him a call. I said, "Hey, Ian. How are you?"

"Fine," he said.

I asked him if he remembered my event, and he said, "I did."

I said, "Well, you didn't show, and I made accommodations for you. I just wanted to make sure, first, that you were okay, but second, I wanted to know why you didn't feel the need to call me and tell me you weren't coming."

He said, "Well, I don't deal with cheaters. How dare you try to pick me up, when you still have a boyfriend back in Texas?" He started going into this tirade about some imaginary man. I didn't know what he was talking about.

Once he got over his attitude—he can be either supersweet, or superfierce (he's a Taurus, sign of the bull)—I told him, "I don't have a man. There is no man."

He said, "Oh? I went to your Facebook page, and it says you're in a relationship."

I started laughing, which of course made him more aggravated. I had never changed my Facebook status—I'm talking, *in years*—and he was going off that.

I said, "Listen. Let's promise each other right now that if we ever have a concern or an issue with the other person, instead of jumping to conclusions, we communicate. We talk about it, no matter how hard it is. I promise you that I will always listen, if you'll always listen to me. I won't jump from my ego or emotions first. I'll talk to you from an empathetic place of trying to understand what you're going through."

He said, "So you're telling me there's no boyfriend?"

I said, "I have two kids, a full-time job, and a mother who lives six minutes away from me in Houston. There is no boyfriend." We giggled. He agreed that we would communicate.

We stayed on the phone for maybe two and a half, three hours after that. We talked about everything. Out of all my relationships, the only one I've ever had that was similar to what I was experiencing with Ian in that moment was the relationship I had with Stephanie when we were kids. We had this sort of best-friend feeling of being able to talk to each other about anything.

Ian and me, the night after my birthday party.

We talked about our lives, our dreams, the things that happened to us as kids. Then he told me he was going to Maine. His mother had been diagnosed with cancer and he needed to go take care of her. He was scared he was going to lose her. I did my best to comfort him and provide him with support.

A few weeks later, I told him I was going back to Texas and that I was worried about how things were going to work with us in different states. Still I said, "Let's just try." At this point, I knew Ian was the man I wanted to build a life with. But after our conversation I realized he had never been in a long-term relationship—I knew we needed to go at a pace that he would be comfortable with.

After that, we talked on the phone every single day for three to four hours. What was so amazing about our relationship, and what made us so strong, was that we started it with a foundation of communication.

There wasn't anything clouding us, like sex or other people trying to influence how we felt or how we behaved. It was just Ian and me, talking. I'm so sad for the younger generation, in some ways, when it comes to the ability to pick up a phone and chat for hours. Everything is so rapid, text-text-text, and if they do get on the phone, it's only for a few minutes.

What built my relationship with Ian were those intimate conversations where I was up, pacing around my bedroom, laughing, going into my kitchen and grabbing something to drink, and trying to mute the phone while I used the restroom, because I didn't want to tell him to pause.

These phone conversations were how we got to know everything about each other. What was also special was that we gave each other space, because we both understood how important family is. We had to put them first. I would say, "I can't talk, because I have to help the children." He would say, "I can't talk, because I'm helping my mom." We would both give each other encouraging words.

Ian is ten years my senior (actually, nine and a half, but I like to round it up to ten, because I know it pisses him off). He's the oldest man I've ever dated, but it's not like he's sixty and I'm twenty-one. He grew up in Portland, Maine, the youngest of six siblings. He was a "surprise" child. His siblings are my parents' age.

When his mother, Carole, found out she was pregnant nine years after she thought she was done having kids, abortion was not an option—she was a religious woman. She made the decision to have the baby, and now she says it's the best decision she ever made. As her other kids were growing up and having their own families, Ian became her best friend and travel buddy.

It was very similar to the relationship I had with my mother—me being the youngest and the only one still in the house. When Ian's father passed, he invited his mom to come to California and hang with him as often as she wanted. He wanted his mother close, which was beautiful to me.

Ian, my mom, Carole, and me, at the lake in Maine in 2018.

We also connected through the fact that Ian's dream growing up was to be a dancer, just like my dream. His mother was a dancer. He always says, "I'm marrying my mother. Both of y'all are show-girls." It's true: when he and his eighty-year-old mother and I get together, boy, do we like to cut up. Any time she comes, she always asks me what the new dance is. When we're dancing together, and I'm teaching her dances like the Stanky Leg, it's the best.

Carole owned a dance studio for almost thirty years. It became a pillar of Portland, Maine. When Ian was taking care of her as she was beating her cancer, one of the nurses was extra careful and attentive. As Ian's mom got stronger, the nurse finally told Carole, "You don't remember me, but I was one of your dance students. When my mother told you she couldn't afford to pay, you told her I could come for free. That's what kept me out of trouble and helped me go to school. The minute I saw your name, I knew I was going to do everything in my power to make sure you got better."

That is just Carole's nature. She's a giver. She's always trying to help people figure themselves out. It's true to some degree that Ian is marrying his mother, and I think that's an honor. If anyone wants to compare me to Carole Jordan, sign me up.

In a sense, I've also married my mother. She is very nurturing, very loving, very strong—but also very opinionated. Which is Ian, a lot of the time. It's like, "I didn't ask your opinion, but thanks for sharing it."

His father was a math teacher and an alcoholic. Ian and I connected through stories of our fathers not being the best role models for us. We both took different routes because of that—he loved his father, and his father was around for him, but as he was growing up, his dad's alcoholism was full-blown.

Because of that, he decided he wasn't going to date anybody, because he didn't want to risk dating anyone similar to his father. I took the opposite path as a serial monogamist; I wanted to find someone and make it work. Those are our personalities even now: the thing Ian says he loves about me is that I like to jump out of a plane first and ask about the parachute next. Ian likes to stay on the ground, and would never even get in the plane. He's too busy trying to figure out all the mechanics of the parachute, the engines, and the pilot. This is what makes us perfect for each other.

After high school, Ian left Maine and moved to New York because he wanted to be a dancer. Someone stifled his dreams, so he gave up and started working in retail until he was almost in his thirties.

That's when he decided he needed a change and moved to California. He got a job as a production assistant, just as a fluke. He moved his way up and eventually became a TV director. I think about what a great example of Ian's personality that is. One of the reasons I fell in love with him is because he didn't give up on life. He tried, he pivoted, and he made a success of himself.

After that first long conversation that we had on the phone, we didn't officially become boyfriends for another three months. Then I asked him if he would be my boyfriend, and he said yes.

We started dating. He was in Maine, and I was making it my priority to move back to California. Ian was one of the first people I told about my dream of being a television host. I knew all the channels that had shows with hosts. I used to put on *E! News*, mute it, put on the closed captioning, and practice using it as if it were my prompter. (The kids would come home and see me doing this and say, "What is wrong with him?")

I told Ian I planned to try for a hosting job at this channel called Reelz. It was all about movies, and I figured that would be a good way to get in. The first thing out of his mouth was, "You don't want to shoot any higher?"

"You fucking asshole," I said. "What do you mean?"

He said, "I just see more for you and your career."

It was a special moment (after I stopped calling him an ass). It was the first time I didn't have somebody telling me that my dream was dumb, or that I couldn't do it. In fact, he was telling me, "Do more! Be better!"

Just a few months into our relationship, he was already pushing me to be more. He was urging me not to settle, in his very sly, sarcastic sort of way—comments that could sound like digs, but were actually words of encouragement. He is very opinionated, which is a quality that I like in men. I also realized that he believed in me from day one. He believed that I could be greater than what I even imagined for myself. His statement only reaffirmed that this was someone I could spend my life with. He is my partner . . . someone I can trust to grow with me.

I remember the first time he did something really sweet. It was a month after my birthday, at Christmastime. Without my knowing, he had sent to my house in Texas these gingerbread cookies with "Jason," "Chris," and "Karamo" written on them. He wrote in a card, "It's a big tradition in my family to have stockings, so I wanted to give you all things for your stockings for you to enjoy." I just thought, *What a thoughtful man to send me and my kids cook-*

ies. At this point, I didn't tell my children they were from Ian. I knew he was The One, but I wasn't telling my children just yet. We didn't visit each other at all during this time—we respected that we both needed to deal with family as we were growing our relationship.

Luckily, his mother recovered from cancer. Ian moved back to California. That summer, once the kids were done with school, I moved back to California as well. We just started dating, dating, dating, dating. We were inseparable.

There are so many things I love about Ian. He has such a great sense of humor and he finds moments to laugh all the time. Everyone in his life says he's the funniest person ever, and he is. He does tell a lot of corny jokes, the kind with a punch line. I don't like those as much—I like it when it's more natural, like when he's just being sweet and funny.

He has three laughs, and I can always tell which laugh it is, and it makes me laugh, too. One is identical to his mother Carole's laugh—it's this sort of higher-pitched *hee, hee, hee.* It's hilarious when they're both doing it at the same time. Then he has this guttural laugh that comes from his stomach—he'll get pissed if I say it's like Santa Claus, but it really *is* a Santa Claus laugh. Like he's flying through the sky with his reindeer. Then he has this third laugh, which is the sweetest one of them all—when he thinks something is really funny, and he's laughing so hard he's almost coughing, and you don't really see his teeth, and his eyes scrunch up and get watery. That's the one that I love the most.

Ian is just so caring. If someone is in need, he is coming to their rescue. Without thinking, he will stop and take care of a family member, a friend, a coworker, or a stranger. If you complain about the sun burning you, he's there with sunscreen. If he wasn't in television, he should have been a doctor or nurse. He has this innate desire to heal people—and he does it without calling attention to himself.

Ian is supportive of . . . let's call them the *unique* parts of my personality. Like the fact that I can't stand when people cut their nails inside the house (I do it outside, always). Or that I do *not* like pain. I have the lowest pain tolerance in the world. I have never broken a bone, never been to the emergency room, because I strategically walk through life making sure I don't get hurt. If I get the lightest prick from a thorn, I'm on the ground, bawling.

When we were taping season 1 of *Queer Eye* in Atlanta, for example, Jonathan Van Ness looked at my ears and said, "Oh, you have hair growing in there." The hairs were so friggin' tiny you could not even see them. He kept saying, "Let's take care of that hair. Come to my house, I'll wax you. No big deal. It's so much nicer than shaving; you won't even feel it."

I said no, but once Jonathan has something in his head, he just keeps pressuring you and pressuring you, in a very funny but relentless way, until you give in and say, "Okay, fine, I'll do it."

I went to his apartment in Atlanta, and he put a little warm wax on my right ear. "See how nice it is?" he asked me.

I thought, *Ooh, okay, this is kind of nice. Maybe this will be fine. I mean, my ear isn't like a hairy chest.* Then Jonathan started yanking on my poor little ear.

I said, "You have to get some oil! Tease it off, don't just rip it off." It took him an hour and fifteen minutes to get the wax off my ear, because I was sobbing. Okay, I can be a bit dramatic. (And afterward, let me point out that there was no hair on the wax.)

I also don't swim. I know how to swim extremely well, but I'm not doing water. Especially community water—like a pool that everyone else has pissed in is the grossest thing ever to me. I'm not doing it. If I have to get into a pool at a party or something, I have to have, like, two Heinekens to ease my nerves. Or just get pushed in.

I love looking at the ocean, but again, that is community water! When I'm at the beach and I see kids coming out of the waves, and they're spitting, and you know people are urinating in the water, the fish are urinating . . . Nope!

I'm a little germaphobic, which, to be honest, is the reason I started giving hugs to people. I don't shake hands very much. When I give hugs, I don't get the germs! That's the reason the guys have started teasing me about my germaphobia. We'd all go to events, and if there was a line of people to meet us, I would start hugging everyone—and even though they'd rather shake hands, they feel obligated to hug, too. (Bobby has started embracing it.)

Ian accepts all those funny quirks about me, as I accept all of him. Communication and acceptance are key ingredients to a healthy relationship.

After I moved back to LA, Ian and I were both in California, inseparable, and fully in love—but there was one awkward moment that could have potentially broken us. I had tattooed the name of my ex-boyfriend—the one who was in a drug spell with me—on my left forearm, in very big bubble letters (that boyfriend also tattooed my name on the back of his leg).

Note to everybody: if you ever tattoo someone's name on you, it's a bad sign. Don't do it. I don't know anybody who's had someone's name tattooed on their body, other than a child's name, who doesn't eventually regret it.

Until that point I had been hiding the tattoo with long-sleeved shirts. I was like, *There is no way he is going to want to stay in a relationship with me when I have another man's name tattooed on my forearm.* We went to a restaurant, and I sat him down. I said, "I have something serious to tell you."

I showed him my forearm, and he was like, "Oh, I saw that on day one! Listen, before we go any further? Get that changed, removed, or covered."

I told him, "Deal. Gotcha."

I got the entire thing covered with a sleeve of a peacock that went down my entire arm.

It took me maybe three months after that to introduce him to the kids. We all went out to dinner. I had told them about Daddy's friend, Mr. Ian. He was a friend who was coming around—but I wouldn't allow him to spend the night, nor would I spend the night at his house. This made intimacy very awkward, because it was like, "The kids have basketball practice—please come over now!" or "I have a lunch break, what are you doing?" But that added a level of excitement to it, too.

Ian and I moved in together in Los Angeles only after four years of dating. By that point, Ian knew the kids and had spent a lot of time with them. They enjoyed "Mr. Ian" coming over and being a part of family time, like dinner and homework.

Having him move in was a big step—one I couldn't make alone. I first talked to Stephanie about it, who was happy that the kids would have another "dad," and he was someone she liked and respected. Then I asked the kids if it was okay. Surprisingly, they were both very cool with it. I think that's because, in part, they never saw me date another guy, so they knew Ian had my heart and was a part of the family. Plus, they loved his cooking.

I loved living with him, but about five years into our relationship, right before *Queer Eye*, I started dropping hints to Ian that marriage was important to me. It was a difficult conversation, because again, our relationship was the first real one that Ian had ever been in. He would say he wasn't sure about marriage when I asked him about it. It made sense, because in our relationship, I was always the one who pulled the trigger on everything: let's communicate; come meet my kids; let's move in together.

Also, I'd been dreaming about what my wedding was going to be like since I was a child. Most of the time, you only hear women say that, but I'm not ashamed to say it. I just kept telling him I would love to be married, but he was very much taking his time.

I would say things to him like, "I've done everything else—this is your job. You ask me to marry you." We had many discussions about his being the one to ask me to marry him. Time passed, and it didn't happen. It became the first point of contention in our relationship. I was like, as the old saying goes, shit or get off the pot. (Now, I had no intention of leaving him, but I needed him to know how serious I was about marriage. Sometimes that's what people who are in love do when they're trying to push their partners to go to the next level. We say things sometimes that we don't mean, because we are hurting.)

I knew my value. I knew my worth, and it was also a priority of mine for my kids to have two parents and a stable, loving house. If he didn't want to give me that, it was time to move on. I was not going to be in a thirty-year relationship where we were still calling each other "boyfriend." To be real here, I stopped calling Ian my boyfriend almost two and a half years into our relationship, because I was embarrassed by that term.

I started calling him little nicknames instead. I call him "Sugah" because he's white and sweet. When I started introducing him to people, I called him Baby Daddy, because they would get a kick out of it. I'd say, "Oh, this is my Baby Daddy," and they'd laugh. I felt like calling him that was no more comical than us being in our thirties and calling each other "boyfriend."

I don't judge anybody who doesn't believe in the institution of marriage. I don't think that needs to be everyone's path, but it was damn sure my path. So I was like, "If this is not your path, then we've gotta move on."

We argued. I remember a month before we finished shooting seasons 1 and 2 of *Queer Eye*, he came to visit me in Atlanta. We went to this restaurant called JCT. I said, "If you don't want to get married, I can't do this." He was anxious, because this was all new to him.

I was like, "I need you to step up." After that, I started getting rumblings from his friends that he was trying to figure out what to do. He was nervous. He knew that getting engaged and getting married were big deals to me.

That was the point where I was literally like, "Fuck it, I'm planning this. I know my man. Even if he decides to plan it, it's gonna be another three years before it happens." In the end, it was not about who did the asking . . . it was about us building a life together. There are no tradition-based "rules" in LGBTQ+ relationships, so we are able to make it work how we see fit.

So I started planning the engagement. I'm the worst at remembering dates, so I try to align all my stuff around the same dates so I won't forget them. The next big date coming up was Ian's birthday, in May 2018, so I thought, *Okay, if I ask him to marry me on his birthday, I will never forget our engagement date.*

I planned a surprise birthday party, which would also serve as the engagement date. I didn't tell anybody I was planning to propose; I just told everyone it was a surprise birthday party. At the time, we were at the height of promoting seasons 1 and 2 of *Queer Eye*. Even though my body was stressed and I was trying to plan a big party, it was still worth it to me. This was a huge moment in my life. Plus, putting too much on my plate is part of my nature. (And then when it's finished, I can say, "See? I told you I had it.")

The day of the party, I had just finished two photo shoots and a press event that started at six in the morning. Our engagement / birthday party was at seven that night.

I got home and orchestrated it perfectly. I said, "Oh, Ian, I made dinner plans, but I'm so tired."

He said, "Baby, we can stay home."

I said, "Okay, let's just stay home." Then I pretended to think about it for a minute, and I said, "You know what? It's your birthday. I can pull it together. Let's just go have a bite, and we can come back."

We got dressed. Ian is a wreck in the closet—I *Queer Eye* him every time we go out. I picked out his clothes, like I always do. I said, "Baby, just wear this." (Because I knew what I wanted him in!) As we were getting dressed, I realized I had forgotten to write the words that I would say to Ian as I asked him to marry me. We got in the car and my mind was swirling: What was I going to say? At the same time, I couldn't let Ian see that I was anxious.

I had told everyone to be there at seven, because we were pulling in at seven thirty on the dot, and I am very punctual. The kids had already left for the party. There were two hundred people attending. I'd flown in his family members; I'd flown in Stephanie. My sons, my family members, and Tre and Ray knew ahead of time that I was going to propose, but everyone else just thought it was a birthday party. My family was supposed to have come, too. Unfortunately, a week before the engagement, my mother had several seizures and went into the hospital. My family was all there, taking care of her. (I wanted to cancel the party, but my mom said that she would be pissed if I didn't follow through.)

I was thankful that at least Ian's family was still going to be at the party. I had rented out this big nightclub on Sunset called Hyde and turned it into a beautiful, lavish party with a DJ and cakes and balloons. I didn't hire anybody—*I* decorated it. (I'm type A; I can't trust anybody else to do it. The kids, Tre, and my friend Lisa were a big help.)

Ian didn't know where we were going. As we were driving, I

said, "Hey, let's be a little fun and kinky. I'm going to blindfold you."

He said, "This is weird, but okay."

So I blindfolded him right before we hit the venue. I had told the maître d' ahead of time to pretend like we had reservations, even though I'd rented out the entire place.

After we entered the restaurant, I took off the blindfold to open Ian's eyes to the sight of two hundred of our closest friends and family members saying "Happy Birthday" as the Stevie Wonder song of the same name played. I'd created this video of all his siblings and my siblings wishing him happy birthday, too. When the video started playing on a big screen, my heart started beating through my chest. I still wasn't sure what I was gonna say to him in the next ten minutes, when I was down on my knee asking him to marry me. While Ian was watching, his family was ushered in behind him. The video ended with me saying, "Sugah, happy birthday. I hope you have a great day, but I have another surprise for you. Turn around."

When he turned around, he saw all his family and he just started bawling.

Another part of the surprise is that after Ian saw his family, my sons then grabbed the mic. They gave a speech, saying, "Dad, we're so happy you found someone." Then they turned to Ian and said, "Our gift to you is that we want to call you Pops." As they delivered their loving words to their soon-to-be-father, they were all crying and hugging. As they talked, I slowly got down on one knee behind Ian. In my mind, I was just thinking, *What if he says no?* Up until that point, I had orchestrated every big moment in our relationship. I still wasn't 100 percent confident that Ian wanted marriage. After my sons finished, they said, "Dad has one more surprise for you."

My sons said, "Pops, can you turn around?" Everyone cheered as Ian did, and he saw me on my knee behind him. Doing what I know how to do best, I began to speak from the heart. I said, "I hope that we can conquer the world together for the rest of our lives. Ian Lamont Jordan, will you marry me?" Then he said, "I will." We fell into each other's arms, tears streaming down both our faces.

With Ian Jordan, the love of my life.

The minute after I asked Ian to marry me, we went outside and called my sister Kamilah, who was with my mom at the hospital. My mother mustered all her strength to tell us how glad she was for us and that she was so happy Ian was going to be a part of the family. (She has since recovered, but her health is something we monitor constantly.)

It was a special night. We're planning our wedding right now—excuse me, *I'm* planning our wedding. It is lavish, lavish, lavish. We're getting married in 2020, because I need enough time to make things perfect. I want all the accoutrements. I want it all!

More than that, I want us to continue to grow together. Ian is the cook in our house—I don't touch a pot in the kitchen. Now, I can cook very well (for the first six years of having the kids, I did all the cooking alone), but it isn't my passion. Ian loves cooking—it's something that relaxes him. I stay away from the kitchen. (Why deprive the man I love of doing something he loves?)

Ian has been crafting a plan on how to help people create diets that are delicious and help their mental health. We've been working together on some projects around it, which is nice. We're getting to a place where not only our lives come together but our passions as well. He's seen the impact I've made on *Queer Eye*, and now he wants to help others feel good about themselves, too.

On the flip side, the kids are now getting older, and they're coming into their own. Jason has said that he wants to get into television, and he's been taking classes at UCLA. I've been so proud of his growth. He's following my lead of making a plan, following the plan, and asking for help when he needs it. I've been telling him not to rush the process and to go at his own pace.

It's so funny. Because I've taken on the role as patriarch of the house and tend to model everything for everyone else, it's sort of trickled down into the way that everyone else thinks. The boys have many viewpoints that are similar to mine. It's a constant reminder that when you're in a house as a parent, or when you're in a sorority house, or a dorm room, or with your friends in a classroom, one person can really set the culture of that space.

———

In my house, everyone is now talking about mental health and being better and stronger. Jason's whole thing now is that he's a comedian and wants to be a comedic actor. Every time he goes into an audition, he says, "Laughter heals people. I want everyone to laugh and heal." That's not something I prompted him to say—it just naturally happened because of the way our household is run.

Jason, Christian, me, and Ian out to dinner.

It's kind of amazing to me that we've become such a strong family. Christian just graduated from high school, and he either wants to be in the fashion industry or a rapper. He's in a space where he wants to help people, too. He hasn't verbalized it like Jason and Ian and I have, because he's younger and having fun, but he's figuring out his life.

We're a happy family. The boys have two dads. Ian's mom, Carole, is so happy that her son met a man who is all about family and love, but who also has kids. Ian became a dad overnight after he met me—and Carole loves the fact that he has added more grandchildren to the family. When she met my kids, she immediately started calling them her grandkids. My extended family was welcoming to Ian when they first met him, too. It was a priority of mine to make sure our families blended.

My Instagram account, the speeches I make around the country, and what I do on *Queer Eye* is such important work to me—to make people understand that they can live better lives. After *Queer Eye*—I mean, I hope that we run forever, but after it ends, I plan on having my own daytime talk show. I'll be a Donahue, or a RuPaul, or a Sally Jessy Raphael for other people.

The dream that I had when I ran for city commissioner when I was a Florida college kid still lives in me as well. I want to help people on a large scale, and I know that I have the motivation and strategic thinking to effect change. In the back of my mind, I still want to be a politician one day. It's always been my dream: As I'm helping people, why not try to create policies to help people live better lives?

With Gavin Newsom, governor-elect of California. I hope to get even more involved in politics.

In 2016, the first time I went to the Obama White House to speak about various policies. I'm in front of all these official people, thinking, *What am I doing here?* While at the same time, thinking, *Hell yes, I'm supposed to be here.*

My badge from the first time I was invited to the White House for work.

My favorite pic with the president during a brunch where we were laughing. He inspires me so much as a father, husband, and politician.

I was invited to speak at the Obama Foundation and got to meet the president.

That's where the talk show comes in, and this book and other books come in, and someday, potentially, my being in politics. I know what it takes to continue to create the life you want for yourself and others. It's the reason I got *Queer Eye*: because I know how to help people, and I'm good at it. That's not ego. That's just true.

I will continue to make sure people know I'm someone they can come to for advice, support, and another thing I think is really important: empathy. I am not judging anyone's journey. When you come from immigrant parents, and you're fighting with your sexuality, and fighting with religion, and addiction, and fighting with being abusive to people, and just fighting to make a good life, you don't have any room to judge anyone. The key thing I want people to know is the reason I help them is that I needed to help myself.

As my family and I go forward, we need to make sure that we continue to be happy and that Ian and I stay strong. To have a happy life, it takes effort. It takes maintenance. It takes gratitude for what you have. It takes checking in with yourself and with others. It takes remembering that modeling the way you want to live doesn't stop when your kids get older.

Happy family: Ian; Jason; our dog, Logan; Christian; and me.

Now, let's not pretend here—the kids still get on my nerves sometimes. That's parenthood. It's stressful and hard. Now that my career is changing, Ian and I always have to communicate more. We have to navigate the time we have with each other. It's a new dynamic.

Even through all of that, I have to remind myself that this was the dream I had as a little boy, when I thought about what I wanted my life to be like as an adult. It's not my dream anymore: it's my reality.

chapter nine

Queer Eye

t was a Sunday night around eleven thirty, and I had just settled down in bed with Ian after a very long and stressful day. I
had just gotten back in town from being in Australia for a month
shooting an MTV series I was hosting called *Are You the One: Second Chances*. It was a matchmaking show where contestants got
the opportunity to win money in the process. Since I had returned
home to California a month prior, every day was filled with playing
catch-up: catching up with the kids, catching up with Ian, catching
up with business partners. I was exhausted.

When I got into bed with Ian, it was like heaven. He was

quickly falling asleep, but it takes my mind a little longer to shut off, so I turned on the TV. I saw that Andy Cohen's *Watch What Happens Live* was on, and the guest was Carson Kressley, one of the stars of the original *Queer Eye* (although back then, it was *Queer Eye for the Straight Guy*). *Watch What Happens Live* is one of my guilty pleasures, because it's fun from beginning to end. Plus, I thought Carson was cool.

I had met Carson one time in my life, which I thought about anytime I saw him on TV. It was 2005, and I had just gotten off *The Real World*, at the age of twenty-four. My season had been nominated for a GLAAD Media Award for accurate and diverse characters on a reality show. GLAAD is an organization that actively monitors the images of lesbian, gay, bisexual, transgender, queer, intersex, and asexual output in print, online, and broadcast media to ensure there is equal and accurate representation of LGBTQ+ individuals.

It was the first time I had ever been nominated for an award, and I was so excited. One of the shows I was up against was the original *Queer Eye*. I was in awe that I was being included in the same category.

When I arrived at the ceremony, it was clear that *Queer Eye* was a hit. Everyone was hounding the original Fab Five on the red carpet. I shyly walked by them and all the press people surrounding them—it was the hottest show on the air. I went straight to my seat. I was too intimidated to say hello.

I was amazed by all the stars walking around. This was such a big moment for a little gay black boy from Texas and Florida. As the night went on, I got more and more nervous. Finally, they got to my category, and I heard, "And the winner is . . . Karamo Brown and Willie Hernandez for *Real World: Philadelphia!*" I ran up onstage along with my *Real World* castmate Willie, feeling emotional and overwhelmed. Before we could get to the mic to speak, however, the award presenter added, "It's actually a tie . . . with the cast of *Queer Eye for the Straight Guy*."

The applause continued again but got even louder as I watched Jai Rodriguez (culture expert), Carson Kressley (fashion expert), Ted Allen (food-and-wine expert), Thom Filicia (design expert), and Kyan Douglas (grooming expert) rise from their seats and join Willie and me onstage. They patiently stood to the side as we made a few remarks.

Then they took the mic, and the crowd erupted in cheers. They made their speech, and then we all went backstage, where Carson made some sort of snarky joke about the award being a tie. You could tell from the reaction of the people backstage that some thought it was funny, while others thought it wasn't. He then came over to me and said, "Good job being gay." I don't know if he was being serious, funny, or shady, but I innocently replied, "Thanks." That was the extent of our conversation.

As I watched Carson on *Watch What Happens Live* talking with Andy—another openly gay celebrity—I was thinking, in the most sincere inner voice, *Good job being gay, guys.* Here were two gay men on national TV, being their authentic selves and showing a generation behind them that success is possible without hiding who you are. In moments like this, I'm reminded of how important visibility is to our community.

As their conversation proceeded, Andy asked the million-dollar question: In a time where many hit shows were being rebooted, would *Queer Eye* ever come back?

To Andy's surprise and mine Carson replied, "Yes it is, but with a new Fab Five."

I immediately perked up in bed and grabbed Ian, who was almost asleep. "Sugah! Sugah!" I screamed. "Did you hear that? They're bringing back *Queer Eye* and casting a new Fab Five. I have to be a part of this reboot."

Exhausted from his day, Ian said something sweet and supportive in a sleepy tone and quickly fell back asleep. But I was wide awake. My mind was swirling with the possibility of auditioning for the reboot of *Queer Eye*.

At that point, I had been hosting television for about three years. I went from my first job of hosting and producing for OWN, the Oprah Winfrey Network, to being a host and producer for *Huffington Post Live* to being a nightly guest host on *Dr. Drew Midday Live*, where I discussed mental health. I'd just wrapped the series with MTV. I felt confident about my ability to be a good host and connect with people on television.

As I sat up in bed thinking about the show, one question kept entering my mind: *Which category would I audition for if I even got the opportunity to be seen?* Design and grooming were immediately out. I'd watched the original show, and there was no way I was going to be able to cut someone's hair or design someone's house. Food and wine? I'm a foodie, but I'm limited to the dishes I know how to prepare. So it was down to fashion and culture. Now, fashion I knew I could do. I have a great sense of style—or so people have told me. I love seeing plays, going to art galleries, and traveling the world, so culture was definitely also an option.

I couldn't stop thinking about it. At 1:00 a.m., I was still wide awake. I opened my computer and searched for old episodes of *Queer Eye*. As I watched the original show, I was reminded of how groundbreaking it was for its time. Five gay men interacting with men from different cultural backgrounds, saying, "We can be friends; we can help you; we aren't that different." Wow. They helped normalize what it was to be a gay man for so many people.

That night I finished one episode, then a second episode, and then a third. I was laughing and enjoying myself—but something was gnawing at me. These men were having beautiful makeovers on the outside—their hair, clothes, home, meals to eat, and events to attend, but no one was focusing on their "inside." Well, maybe Ted Allen did, literally—he was the food-and-wine expert and was showing them how to change their diet—but that was it. As a fan of the show, I felt cheated that we only briefly got to see these men talk about what emotionally and mentally had been holding them back. A guy getting a makeover would say, "I haven't cut my hair in twenty years, and that was also the last time I dated." No one dug deeper. No one asked, "Why? Why haven't you cut your hair in twenty years? Why haven't you dated in twenty years? What are you scared of? What is blocking you?"

There was no, "Let's get to the emotional and mental core of why you're living your life this way." It was always, "Well, we fixed the outside, so all will be well."

This is by no means a slight or an attack on the original show. It was a different time, and I'm sure the network demanded only light and fun content. But it's a different day—and I know that just fixing the exterior is not enough for long-lasting change. You also have to focus on emotional and mental health if you truly want a successful life. To take better care of yourself, you need to get to the root of your emotional blocks.

In my past line of work as a social worker and psychotherapist, empathetic listening and guiding people to the emotional core of their issues is critical. I've learned how to become a blank slate, maintaining a posture of reticence and neutrality, so as not to inter- fere with the workings of a person's subconscious. I've learned how to ask questions in a way that makes whomever I'm speaking with see me as the person they need me to be in that moment, in order to reveal the source of their distress.

Yet this was not occurring in any of the episodes I had just watched. Late that night, I figured out what my role on the show was going to be before even finding out how I could audition. I was going to try to be the show's psychotherapist / life coach / emotional mentor: whatever you want to call the person who fixes the inside, that's who I wanted to be.

That morning, I called my amazing agent, Tyler Kroos, and told him that *Queer Eye* was coming back to TV and that I had to be a part of the show. Of course, his first question was, "Which category do you want to audition for, if we can get you in?"

When I told him I wanted to be the show's therapist, there was a long pause. Then Tyler began reminding me of what the five categories were. "How about we try to get you an audition for culture, and from there you can craft it into what you want?" he suggested. Of course, I agreed.

A few days later, Tyler called back. "Sorry, Karamo," he said, "but it looks like you decided to audition too late." The production company had already finalized casting, and they were bringing the top forty contenders to LA in a few weeks to do a chemistry test—an evaluation of how two or more people interact with one another in an audition—before selecting the new Fab Five.

I was devastated when I received the news. Then Tyler said something that changed the trajectory of my life forever.

"I know the senior vice president of casting, Gretchen Palek," Tyler said, "and I am going to hard-pitch you to her. I'm going to see if she will take a chance on you and slide you in for an audition before the chemistry test. I believe in you, and I know that if they see you, you'll get this job." I was overwhelmed and humbled by his efforts.

Even though it was still a long shot, I started preparing for the audition. A few days later, Tyler called me and said, "Gretchen agreed to audition you . . . but you only get one chance! They're busy setting up activities for the chemistry test, so they don't have a lot of time to get to know you." Tyler asked me how I felt about that, and I simply said, "I got this."

I hung up the phone and walked down the hallway of my apartment, into my bedroom, and then into my bathroom. I closed the door behind me and looked in the mirror and said to myself, "I *don't* got this." It's funny now, but in that moment, I was terrified.

One shot. That's a lot of pressure. I wasn't even sure how I was going to sell them on me being the culture guy. Based on what the culture-expert role was on the original show, they were looking for someone who knew everything about museums, art, and plays. Don't get me wrong—Tchaikovsky's *Swan Lake* is my favorite ballet, I love exploring the Louvre any time I'm in Paris, and I have attended dozens of Broadway plays in New York City . . . but that doesn't make me an expert in any of those fields.

In that moment, I was riddled with anxiety and plagued by internal conflict. On the one hand, I was getting the audition of a lifetime. On the other, I had no idea how I was going to convince the casting agents in one meeting that culture should really be life coaching. I could just picture myself walking into that room, pitch ready to go:

Hi, I know we are just meeting for the first time, but I think you're making a big mistake by making the culture category about the arts and not about emotional and mental growth. Can you please overhaul the whole category? And hire me, while you're at it?

Sounds crazy, right?

I walked out of the bathroom and sat on my bed. Near the edge was a teddy bear that Ian had given me on Valentine's Day a few years back. The teddy bear (who I'd affectionately named Charles) was holding a heart that read, "I love you." Looking at Charles, I started to feel not so alone and began remembering why I even decided to follow my dreams in the first place. These opportunities and auditions were for myself, but they were also so I could provide a better life for my family and for people in general. I fell into a trance looking at Charles, thinking, *You can figure this out.* I kept repeating in my mind, *I love myself, my family loves me, and these casting directors can love me, too.*

After talking myself out of the self-doubt that was threatening to cloud my mind, I hopped up, grabbed my computer, and headed to the dining room table. I was going to show these casting directors that I Am Culture. I opened a blank page in Microsoft Word and at the top wrote just that: Why I Am Culture.

I decided that with only one shot to impress the casting director, I couldn't sell a skill, such as experience in design and fashion. Instead, I needed to sell *me*.

One thing I have learned throughout my life is that what interests people most isn't your degree or your brand or product: it's you. I knew that showing every part of myself in that audition, and being open to sharing my story, was the first step I needed to take.

With a Word page open in front of me, I started thinking critically about my life from its beginning and key things that I wanted to share. I began to write down facts, such as that my family is Jamaican-Cuban. I wrote down that I was from the South, had attended an HBCU (historically black college/university), and found out I was a father in my early twenties.

I typed for four or five hours. Once I had my list, I started realizing that so many parts of my life had been culture-focused. I'd spent so much time learning from people in different places, experiencing different ideas and points of view, from school to clubs to my social work, and understanding that life is bigger than just my four walls.

I also realized that, as a former social worker, I had been trained to have culturally relevant conversations with people—in fact, it was one of my greatest gifts. Helping people understand how to have hard conversations with themselves so that they can later have hard conversations with others is something I excel at. I knew that I had a shot of making it to the chemistry test if I was able to tell casting that having culturally relevant conversations is important.

The morning of my audition, I anxiously waited in front of the computer at 9:59 a.m. for my 10:00 a.m. Skype meeting. At that point, I felt as comfortable as I was going to feel. I just kept telling myself that all I needed to do in that moment was to have fun and be myself.

That is something I had practiced a lot over the years—being myself in tough situations. I did what I always did when those moments arose: I took a couple deep breaths and reminded myself that this moment was essentially me just sharing my life—and that no one else could do that better than me.

The clock struck ten and I started to hear the Skype incoming-call noise. My heart began beating fast, and I took a deep breath as I pressed the button to answer. I saw a visual in my screen, and I was greeted by a young woman in her midtwenties who was smiling and sitting in a conference room. I had assumed that there would probably be five or six people on this call listening in and judging me based on what I said, how I looked, and what I did. But that wasn't the case: there was just this woman on one end of the call and me on the other.

This is something I can thrive on, I told myself. I had spent my career connecting with people on a one-on-one basis—from peer counseling in high school to my professional life. I always got excited when it was just myself and my client in my office, because I knew we were about to figure out what was bothering them so that they could grow. One-on-one is where I have the most real and authentic conversations, and where I feel most at home. Even though it was on Skype, we could make a real connection.

We began talking quickly about *Queer Eye* and how I could possibly fit into the puzzle. She asked me a couple questions, and I decided at that moment that we were going to have a conversation, not do an interview. Just as much as she was getting to know me, I was going to give her room to insert who she was into the conversation as well. It would give us an opportunity to have an authentic moment—where she really got to know me and I really got to know her. I wanted to show her that I was somebody who could be her friend. I could do this job and connect with people around the country in the same easy way.

I remember the first real question after the small talk was "Tell me about yourself." I was prepared. Soon she was at ease, and so was I. We were having a conversation as if we were two old friends talking about our lives. Of course, this whole process was strategic. At no point did I get overly comfortable—where I might forget that this was still an interview. At the end of that call, a decision was going to be made whether I was going to have the opportunity to move on to the next round or not. Still, I wanted to make sure the process felt authentic to me—the same thing I wanted for the show.

Then came the question "What does culture mean to you?" Without hesitation, I answered proudly, "I am culture." I didn't say it arrogantly, but in a way that showed her I was serious about the job. I then followed up with facts from my own life to back up why I was the future culture expert.

The definition of culture is the customary beliefs, social forms, and material traits of a racial, religious, or social group. It's also defined as a set of shared attitudes, values, goals, and practices that characterizes an institution, organization, or person. Everything described in this definition is about the emotions, feelings, hopes, and desires that people and communities hold close and pass on to future generations. Nothing specifically about art or plays or museums. Culture is about what people feel, and how they experience the world around them.

I used this definition as my baseline for why I am culture. You can't be a young, gay African-American man, growing up in the South with immigrant parents, living in majority-white neighborhoods, attending a historically black college, working as a social worker and psychotherapist, and working with people from all different backgrounds without understanding the importance of shared attitudes, values, and beliefs—and how the labels the world puts on us affect us in negative or positive ways.

At this point I slipped in the fact that I believed that culturally relevant conversations were a crucial element in a makeover, because they would allow the person to have real growth. Making over your inside is just as important as making over your outside.

I saw her eyes light up at this, and she asked me to tell her more. I went into the fact that for people to maintain exterior change, they had to have an equal or greater internal change. I illustrated how internal changes give people the ability to evaluate and understand why they didn't make that change before, and how they can maintain that change in the future. Then we started talking about how I had done this in my career, and I listed for her all the many times that I had done it with clients, with my fiancé, with my children, and for myself.

I could see she was intrigued. She told me that the call had been recorded and that she would be sharing it with other people in her department. She also said they would decide very quickly whether they would be inviting me to the next round. I thanked her for her time and her candor, and for giving me the opportunity. We hung up, and I melted into the back of my seat and let out a big sigh of relief.

I had done all that I could to show that I was dedicated and experienced, that I wanted this job and knew I could do it. It was now out of my hands. There was nothing I could do until I got a call from my agent. I closed my computer, got in my car, and went for a celebratory lunch at Granville, my favorite restaurant in Los Angeles. Then I just enjoyed the rest of my day. This is a technique I teach my clients, my kids, and even Ian: when you've done all you can do in a certain situation, it doesn't help you at all to stress over it or overthink it—it's done. Anytime the worry about the position would pop into my head, I'd quickly quiet those thoughts by focusing on something that made me happy. It's all about shifting your energy and attention.

After about a week of trying not to think about the situation, it happened. My phone rang. It was my agent, Tyler. My heart hammered in my chest as I picked up the phone. "Hey, Karamo, I have some news for you about the audition," Tyler said. "I heard from Gretchen, and she and her team were impressed with you and want to bring you in for the chemistry test."

I stood still for a second in disbelief. Then I started screaming. I had made it to the next round based on just being me and not trying to pretend I was anything but myself. I couldn't believe that I had gotten this opportunity through that approach alone.

I thanked Tyler for fighting for me when he could've easily said, "Well, the opportunity has passed." Celebration aside, I knew this was where the real work started, because I had a different agenda for the culture category. I had to convince others that it could actually work.

The chemistry test was held two weeks later in a hotel ballroom in Burbank, California. It was conducted over three days. During that time, the casting directors and producers would be making cuts. Candidates would be sent home immediately from each of the different categories if they did not have chemistry with the other guys. The pressure was on, but I just kept telling myself, *I've done it once based on who I am, and that's all I need to do in this moment as well.*

I knew that I'd be nervous no matter what, so I wanted to get an outfit that would make me feel confident when walking into that room. (Looking back on it now, that's a similar mind-set we have on *Queer Eye* when it comes to approaching fashion.) I went to the mall and picked up this amazing Diesel bomber that had orange, blue, and yellow stripes on it. I wanted the casting directors to see not only my style but also that I was sporting gay-flag colors to some degree. I also picked up a second and third outfit. I told myself that I was going to be there for all three days, so I needed three outfits. That was me putting it out in the universe that I had this.

The first night of chemistry testing came around. They disguised it as a meet and greet for all the candidates to mingle at a bar with one another before we started the casting process. I knew that this was no social event—this was the first time the executives were going to see our personalities interacting with other people's. It was my job to get into that room and learn about as many people as I possibly could. This was my chance to show people that the culture category could be something more than it had been the first time around.

By the end of that night, I had connected with everyone in the room on a very real level. Each person had shared with me something intimate about his life. One thing quickly became very apparent—everyone who was there for the culture category had either been musical, been a ballet dancer, owned their own art gallery, or done something in the arts. There was only one other guy I met who was a life coach. He must have had a similar idea about what was missing from the original show.

When I met him, he was a nice guy but he seemed a little shy and guarded. I reminded myself that the only person I was in competition with was Karamo. (But that didn't mean I couldn't keep my side eye on him to see what he was saying and doing. Hey, I'm focused but not foolish.)

The next day, we started the chemistry tests bright and early in the hotel lobby. The casting team put all the candidates in a ballroom. They told us that people would be leaving throughout the process until there were ten contestants left—two for each category.

Within the first few minutes of being in the ballroom, I connected with Bobby and Tan. We were drawn to one another. There was a warm, kind, and friendly energy immediately present among all three of us. I could tell we would become friends quickly. Bobby was the very first person I had spoken to at the meet and greet, and I remember thinking, *He is a hustler.* He was discussing his plan to make this opportunity happen. He shared that he had had somewhat of a hard life, but he wasn't going to let that stop him. I saw a lot of myself in him.

Tan was polite but direct. He invited Bobby and me to sit with him and then demanded we share our stories. As we opened up, so did he. You could see his heart and sense of humor right away. No matter the temperature, I'm always cold, and within minutes I was wearing Tan's jacket, which he graciously loaned me.

Jonathan was next to come over. If I can be honest, I had a crush on him when I first saw him. He has a big personality, and that first meeting was no different. He walked over and said, "What are you girls talking about?" We shared a bit and then his personality shifted, and I heard this brilliant man speak. There was no "Yass" or "Hi, queens," just this encyclopedia of lessons he had learned about how to be happy with life and with himself.

Antoni Porowski was last to join our group. He was, and still is, hard to read. He's always in his head overanalyzing every situation and his actions in those situations. But as he joined us, I could feel the same ease come over him. He relaxed, as if he knew he wasn't being judged by us, which allowed him to open up.

During our first interaction, none of us talked about our skill set or the category we were auditioning for. We connected on a human level . . . just wanting to be seen, accepted, and safe. Even though we were all auditioning, we had organically found one another and started bonding right away. What I think is most special about this situation is that we immediately and genuinely wanted to support one another throughout the process.

They began calling us one by one into the room adjacent to the ballroom to ask us questions. When one of the five of us got called in, we would tell the other four what had just happened once we came back out. This was not typical of the other guys they were auditioning. The majority of them would go into the room, come out, and keep whatever happened close to their chests. They didn't want to share the information they had received with anyone else, as if they were scared that they would give someone else a competitive edge. But the five of us didn't feel that way. We felt from the beginning that it would be better if we helped one another—then possibly somebody we knew and liked could be cast for the show.

In the audition room, the producers asked us questions about ourselves and gave us hypothetical scenarios, and they watched us interact with one another. By the end of the day, we went from about forty contestants to about twenty. I was excited that I had made it past the first rounds of cuts. I was also extremely happy to see that the other four guys were still there as well.

Before the day ended, the five of us decided to exchange telephone numbers. Bobby started a group text chat that he titled "The Fab Five." It was either completely delusional of him or completely clairvoyant. Either way, we knew that we would be lifelong friends.

On day two, the organizers had set up a number of games and activities for us to do. In one round, we were led over to a room with five or six tables. At each table there was a fishbowl with slips of paper inside and questions written on them. You had to reach in, pick out a question, and just start talking—I remember one question was "What was your coming-out experience?"

By day three, I was so busy trying to do my best that I wasn't even paying attention to the other guys leaving. Then I realized that there were only about ten guys left. As the reality of this moment set in, I looked around and my heart began to smile. I saw that my original four friends, Bobby, Antoni, Tan, and Jonathan, had made it to the final ten, too. We were hanging out the entire time—the bond was there from the first day and continued on. But this wasn't sleepover camp. We were auditioning, so most of our interactions took place as we were going in and out of rooms.

The producers then split us up into two groups of five—one group went to one house, and the other group went to another house. My group was told we were going to one of the show creator's houses. This person didn't live too far away from the hotel. We were actually going to tape a mini episode. It was about eight o'clock at night after we had just spent a full day auditioning, but that didn't matter. Once we got in the van to ride over there, I was in game mode. They wanted to throw us into the lion's den and see what we would do with cameras on—could we be relaxed and engaging in a stranger's home?

I went into a quiet corner in the ballroom to prepare myself mentally before we left. A young lady who was working for the show came over and asked how I was doing. I told her I was great but was trying to prepare mentally for the next step in the audition. She moved closer to me and put her hand on my shoulder. Leaning in so no one else could hear her, she said, "Can I give you a piece of advice? You're great, and everyone loves you, but maybe you should start talking about plays and the arts more, if you want a shot at this job."

My heart sank into my chest. I thought, *I have blown it*. This conflict of wanting to follow my heart versus what was clearly laid out in front of me was about to cost me my dream opportunity. I asked why she felt this way. She just shrugged and said, "I hear things."

Shortly after this brief conversation, they told each group of five to head to the front of the hotel. The cars would be waiting to take us to the houses to film. My mind was in turmoil. This was the final step in the casting process, and I had to make a decision: either talk about museums and art, or try to help a stranger get to their emotional core. On the entire drive there, I was quiet. I had a choice to make, and I had to make it quickly.

We arrived at the house. I knew I had to get out of my head and back in the game. My group entered the house full of energy. We were giving it our all as we explored and discovered everything we could. This was fine for me. I was being myself, talking to the camera and the other guys, and just enjoying it all.

Then we were told that we were each going to have a one-on-one with the owner of the house, a.k.a. the show creator's husband. The cameraman signaled to me that it was my turn to talk to him alone. I still hadn't decided what I was going to do.

I sat down with him in his study, with him on his couch and me in a chair next to him. I thought to myself, *Getting this far in the process must be a sign from God. Be you, Karamo. You're in a setting similar to your therapy sessions—just do what you've always done.* I began asking him questions about his life, why he needed our help, what he was most afraid of, what brought him the most joy, when was the last time that he had felt really good about himself.

He wasn't responding. I was falling flat.

I realized my questions were not going anywhere because he was acting. I'd had a similar experience with another actor the day before. The information we had about this guy was fake, and he was essentially playing a character—so of course he was not having an emotional response to anything I was saying! He would just respond yes or no.

At that point, I was scared. I didn't want it to show on my face, so I just continued on as if everything was okay. I thought, *I've made it this far, so they must've seen something in me—but now this is the finish line. Maybe I can salvage my chances and end by asking him about a museum or play.* But before I could ask another question, they told me my time was up. They ushered him to another room to meet with one of the other guys.

After ten minutes, they told all of us that the audition was complete and we should get back in the car. Then they took us back to the hotel and dropped us off. They said they'd be making their decisions very quickly. We would be getting a call informing us whether we made it.

On the car ride home, I was freaking out. In my mind, I had

reached the finish line but didn't end strong. I worried that listening to my gut hadn't paid off. I kept replaying what that woman had said to me in the ballroom. She was trying to warn me, but I was stubborn. Now it was too late: the audition was over.

By the time I arrived at my house, I had calmed down. I told myself, *Karamo, you've done everything you can do, and now it's in someone else's hands. If this opportunity is yours it was meant for you. If it's not, then you will be happy for whoever else gets this.* I decided to forgive myself. I've learned over the years that we become emotional wrecks when we don't forgive ourselves for the things in our lives that we couldn't control or that didn't turn out the way we wanted them to. So it was important to let it go. I had stayed true to myself. That is all that matters.

Two weeks went by. None of us on the Fab Five text chain had gotten any word about who was cast. In the meantime, I had gone to Miami to teach at a conference on television hosting. I had decided that since I had some free time, I would help aspiring television hosts learn the craft of being in front of a camera. I wanted to give back and share the knowledge I had gained over the past three years so that they might not make the same mistakes I made when I first started out.

At 8:00 p.m., while I was in the middle of teaching students about maintaining an on-camera presence, my phone rang. It was a Los Angeles number that wasn't recognized by my phone, and this was odd to me, because I don't get a lot of calls. That's the thing about being in a monogamous relationship and being a father—when my phone rings, it's usually only my kids, Ian, my mom, my sisters, and every once in a while a friend checking in to see how I'm doing. This moment sent chills down my spine. I told the class, "Excuse me, but I have to take this." I ran outside and answered the call.

On the other line were the show creators. They started off by telling me what a good job I had done and that they were excited they'd had the opportunity to meet me. They told me in a serious tone that this had been a very hard decision. Unfortunately not everyone made the cut, but they were thankful for how we had given it our all. As they were saying this, I was thinking to myself, *They're telling me I didn't make it.* At the same time, as I allowed these self-doubting thoughts to enter my mind, the producers said in unison, "But you're not one of the contestants who didn't make the cut! Congratulations, you're a member of the new Fab Five!"

I screamed and started running around the empty parking lot where the conference was being held. I had wanted this life-changing opportunity so badly, and I thought I might have possibly ruined my chances by following my intuition. *Queer Eye* was the culmination of everything I had worked so hard for over the course of my life—an opportunity to launch my career and bring me into a space where people could see me as an authority on self-improvement and as a trusted friend.

They told me not to say anything to anyone, because it was

confidential. They also said they hadn't told any of the other guys yet, and they didn't want me to get them all worked up. Of course I agreed that I wouldn't tell anyone—while simultaneously texting the other guys in the Fab Five group chat. I told them I had just gotten the call that I had made it, so they should be finding out soon.

Over the next thirty minutes, each of us on the text chain chimed in one by one, saying "I made it." "I made it, too." "Me three." The only one of us who didn't chime in was Antoni, who still hadn't gotten a call. Apparently there was some conflict at the network with someone who wanted one person, and another who wanted Antoni.

This was rough for us. Four of us had made it, but we were determined to make sure that Antoni's confidence never wavered. We were going to support him as we went through this. They told us that we were going to do yet another round of auditions in the next couple days, but this time just for the food-and-wine category, so they could make their decision.

As much as I was thinking about Antoni and wanting to support him, I also knew that there would still be a conflict with what the producers wanted the culture expert role to be versus what I knew it should be. So I saw this as an opportunity for me to basically convince the producers that I could get to the emotional-core issue of whoever we were helping. I wanted to prove myself and my vision.

Two days later, they brought the four of us to this guy's house in Glendale, California. They set up a scenario for the four of us—plus five different food-and-wine experts (including Antoni). They planned to film five mini episodes to see how we interacted with each food candidate. Again, the guy we were helping was an actor—someone the production team had brought in. Once again, there was no way for me to really show my skills because here we were making over an actor who was playing the role of not really being open to change. This was frustrating for me, because the other guys could talk about his house, his clothes, his hair, and his diet . . . but I needed this gentleman to be open enough for me to have a culturally relevant conversation with him about his issues. Helping people grow internally isn't magic. You can't put a spell on someone and have them figure everything out. For me to work with them, it takes someone being willing to explore their emotions and thoughts.

We walked into the house with the first food-and-wine candidate. As we were exploring, I saw that there was a child's room. I looked around and noticed that the child had been isolating himself in there, because of the way things were set up. It was obvious to me. We also found out right then that the child's mother had just passed. Trying to make some sort of assessment, I made a statement about the child being isolated.

As we finished that scene, and before we started to film the next mini episode with the second food-and-wine guy, one of the creators of the show came up to me. He said, "Hey, Karamo, so I think you should cut all the therapy stuff from now on and talk more about the arts in ways that can encourage a person to have a new experience."

I had blown it. Not that I had lost the job (the job was officially mine) but now I had confirmation that I shouldn't help people get an emotional makeover. Being told I could not do what I knew in my soul was what the show needed to elevate it to the next level was a devastating experience. But I decided to try again. Having three years of experience in television, I knew that once we got to Atlanta to begin shooting season 1, I would have a real opportunity to help someone. After all, the people on the show weren't going to be actors, and we would be shooting sixteen back-to-back episodes over the course of four months. That was plenty of time to make a difference in at least one person's life.

I know what you're thinking: *Karamo is stubborn, extremely hardheaded, and maybe a little defiant.* And you are right, kinda. My middle name does mean "rebel," and when my intuition tells me that I should be doing more—fighting for more, pushing the conversation forward more—I can't help but listen to it.

Thankfully, after the third audition of food-and-wine experts, Antoni was cast. The new Fab Five was complete. I still sometimes can't believe that the guys I connected with on the first day of casting became the men I get to go on this journey with. I guess it was kismet.

My brothers, the Fab Five: Tan, Antoni, Jonathan, me, and Bobby.

We filmed the first and second seasons in Atlanta (eight shows for season 1, and eight for season 2). On the night before we started filming the first episode, I was on the phone with Ian all night. I was nervous, because I was conflicted. I was getting one message from one of the show's bosses and another message from my true bosses—my heart, my soul, and my intuition. Ian, always in my corner and knowing what I was capable of, told me to listen to my true bosses.

The next morning as I woke up, I decided I was going to follow my heart. If they got upset and fired me, at least I got fired for doing what I felt was best. (Although don't get me wrong: by no means did I want to lose my job.)

Our first hero we met was Tom Jackson. He was in his fifties and lived in a small bedroom in someone else's home. He was divorced and had very low self-esteem. He kept saying to us, "You can't fix ugly." I knew this was my opportunity to show what I could do.

The producers preplanned that I would help Tom learn how to date again. They wanted me to take him to a store where he could learn how to flirt and talk to women. Of course, I was not going to go against what they had planned, but I couldn't help but think, *How can I help him to understand why he's having these self-esteem issues, and give him the tools to overcome them?*

Every time Tom and I were alone, we would have these deep, heartfelt one-on-one conversations—sometimes the camera was there and other times, it wasn't. I tried to get him to a place where he could see who he truly was through our work. I asked him, "What story are you telling yourself and others about you? Think about the jokes you make about yourself, the way you receive or don't receive a compliment, the way you walk into a room."

Once he identified that, I told him it was time to start writing a new story. Along with that, I told him it was important to avoid falling into the trap of comparing himself with others' stories. That was causing him to have lower self-esteem. I made him repeat the mantra, "I love me and this is why. . . ." Then he would fill in the blank with three things.

It was incredibly rewarding to see Tom's breakthrough, but none of the life coaching I did with him made that first episode. Some crew members with keen eyes did notice that each time Tom was around me, he got excited and very happy. They also noticed that at the end of the episode—once I started speaking to him—he started crying immediately. I'm not arrogant enough to suggest that his entire transformation was due to me, because it wasn't. My brothers are geniuses at what they do. But I can acknowledge that a big piece of what allowed Tom to truly see himself in a different way was because of the long talks we had, and the tools I gave him to help him grow emotionally and mentally.

I kept letting him know throughout filming that he was a beautiful man and asked him to repeat it after me. I also helped him to understand when his low self-esteem started—when he began giving up on himself. What he and I discovered is that it all started when his ex-wife left him. That's when he lost his drive to see himself as desirable and worthy. The episode never showed any of that because it went a different way. I was supposed to give him confidence to start dating again, but halfway through the taping, he decided he had gained the confidence to call his ex-wife and ask her out again. It was something I supported him on, but the audience never got to see the buildup to that moment.

Because of how Tom's episode ultimately ended up, all the ways I was teaching him to feel good about dating suddenly didn't make any sense, so that got cut, too. I was drastically cut out of the very first episode, because the activity I did with Tom didn't make any sense for the story anymore. Some people could see that something in our interaction was helping him to grow and find himself in a different way, and Tom's emotional breakthrough was all the confirmation I needed to know that I was doing the right thing with the culture category.

By the second and third episodes, it became a recurring joke with the Fab Five that when the heroes got around me, they were going to start crying. That's when Bobby nicknamed me "Kar-Oprah," because I would end up having these long, deep conversations that would get the men we were making over to break down and start crying in my arms. Although I was doing this, I was still getting feedback from behind the scenes that I needed to be doing things like making photo albums and taking people to dance classes—in other words, doing activities that represented "culture."

I went along with it, because after being told during the second round of casting that life coaching and therapy had no place in the show, I didn't dare to bring up what I was doing. I was just going to do what was asked of me, while still finding stolen moments to have deeper, culturally relevant conversations with the men we were helping.

We shot sixteen episodes back-to-back over the summer of 2017. We spent four months in Atlanta and around Georgia, shooting week after week. By the time we had gotten to episode four or five, I was confident in my ability to get to the emotional core of what our heroes were going through. But I was still getting feedback from the higher-ups (not the network) that I needed to be doing more culture-related activities with the heroes.

I understand fully why it was a point of contention for everyone. *Queer Eye* is a visual show where the audience gets to see the change our hero is experiencing. People want to see the hero's hair change, see their wardrobe change, see the food on their plate change, and see their house change. But how do you see their "culture" change when it's about their inner emotions?

The producers wanted something visual, and the tears that were coming from our heroes were not enough. So in season 1, you see me making photo albums, planning an engagement, being a dancer, tasting whiskey. I basically became a chameleon in order to show a "cultural experience," when all I really wanted to do was just sit down and have a conversation.

Eventually, I found a way around it in my car rides with our heroes. When I got into the car alone with the person we were helping that week, there were no producers around and no activities to do—it was just me and the person talking. I knew that this was my opportunity to get them to open up to me about what was going on in their hearts and their minds, without having to sneak a moment in between some activity I was being encouraged to do with them.

These car rides were my favorite thing to do while shooting, because it was my opportunity to help our heroes figure out why they were living the way they were living, and make positive changes toward a better life. I'd ask how their pasts had led them to their current paths. Once we were in the car we went in deep—I wanted to make sure the external makeovers they were getting would last.

After the first season wrapped, I knew I had given it my all. But I also knew from the rumblings of people on the crew and the higher-ups that they weren't sure how I was going to be edited. The editors had to piece together each episode, taking sixty hours of footage from each individual shoot and turning it into a fifty-four-minute show.

I decided not to stress over it and to pray for the best. A couple of times when I visited New York, I met with the editors who were cutting the show. One said, "Every time you get into a car with someone, we all joke, 'Here come the tears.'" That made me happy: a cathartic cry was the first step of watering the seeds of growth within each person we met on the way.

I was optimistic. I had stuck to my guns without discussing it with anyone, and I had faith it was going to turn out great.

Then the network told us that the show would be released in early February 2018. They sent us a link so that we could watch the first eight episodes before anyone else saw them. I gathered Ian and my sons around so we could watch it together.

As we began watching the first episode, "You Can't Fix Ugly," my heart sank. All the emotional and mental work I had done with Tom had been cut out. For the most part, I wasn't even in the first episode. My kids looked at me, confused as to why I wasn't featured more. To be honest, I was embarrassed. We watched the rest of the episodes. There were glimpses of where you could see what I was trying to do. But after all that work I did during the shoot itself, you couldn't really tell that I was trying to fix the inside while everyone else fixed the outside because of the way the editing had been done.

It seemed like I had eight different jobs, because I went from whiskey tasting to doing extreme sports to being a dating expert to making a photo album. Within all that, there were some really amazing emotional moments. I was scared that viewers wouldn't understand why those emotional moments were happening, since most of the work I was doing wasn't shown. After watching all eight episodes I turned off the TV. I never talked about season 1 again to anyone in my personal life.

To this day, I have seen season 1 of *Queer Eye* only that one time. It's painful for me. I was trying to fight for something I knew needed to be there but that really wasn't showing up the way that I'd hoped.

Let me be very honest: I don't think this is the network's fault, I don't think it's the creators' fault, and I definitely don't think it's the editors' fault. In hindsight, I realize the disconnect happened because I should have asked everyone to come together to have a clear conversation about what I saw my category being. I should have asked how we could work together to make my goal a reality. Instead I tried to do it on my own, fighting against what random people had said over the course of auditioning.

I had done myself a disservice. I know that communication is key in any successful relationship, and it's the key in dealing with conflict. Yet I never stopped to make sure that we were all on the same page when it came to my category.

The show aired. Just as I feared, the majority of reviews that came in from both fans and press said that the show was great, but they had no idea what the culture category did. This hurt my heart more than I can explain. I'd just spent the past five months building other people's self-esteem, but my self-esteem was diminishing each day the show was out. This was supposed to be one of the most exciting times in my life. I was devastated because people didn't understand who I was and what I was on the show to do. I felt like an outsider on my own show.

The only person I would talk to about this besides Ian was Bobby. Bobby and I had gotten really close during this time. I could open up to him about what I was feeling and he could do the same with me. To add insult to injury, articles and fan comments started coming out about who among the Fab Five was most attractive, who was most talented, and who was the best.

It's even hard to write this and relive it—a few tears are falling from my eyes as I type. I was fighting this internal conflict to believe in myself again, but the negative voices from the press and social media were winning. All I could think about was the fact that people kept saying, "What's the purpose of the culture category?" Or, "I don't understand Karamo's role on the show."

I finally got myself back to a place where I remembered that I was doing this to help others. The media and viewer opinions of me didn't matter so long as the opinion of the person I helped during the taping was positive. One by one, I started receiving messages from the first eight heroes we had made over. They told me how the time I had spent with them had changed them forever. Hearing them say that I had gotten them to have an emotional breakthrough was the best reminder of what I was on this show— and this planet—to do.

Gradually, my faith in myself and in what I could do on the show ended up manifesting. After the show had been out for about a month, I started to see a shift in the press comments written about me. They saw that I was making substantial changes in people's lives. In articles, writers were starting to say things like, "When Karamo gets on the screen, be prepared to cry" or "Why are they calling Karamo 'culture' and not 'the world's therapist'?" I could even see the change on my social media. People started asking me if I would be their therapist or life coach, and calling me "Dad."

This is a lesson I try to share with people all the time. Sometimes when negative voices start to penetrate into your mind, you have to go back to the core of who you are and why you do the things you do. If you allow people to dictate your self-esteem based on their opinions of you, you will always fail. So for me, in this moment, it was about remembering why I was on the show. Was I on there for fame? That was a by-product, of course, but the main answer is no. Was I on there for a big social media following? Again, no.

The guys and me after taking a swim. Love our private moments.

I kept reminding myself that the reason I wanted to be on *Queer Eye* in the first place was to help people grow and to have better relationships with themselves and those around them.

Then season 2 came out, and you could see more of what I was doing with my category. I don't know if there was a re-edit or if I was just better at conveying my role since we had been filming for so long at that point. But during the second season people really started to get what I was trying to do.

As the show became more popular, and the Fab Five traveled the globe together to do more press, I found time to have conversations with the show's higher-ups about what I wanted my role to be and how we could work together to really make that happen. Of course they were all on board. They asked why I didn't come to them earlier. I was candid. I shared my experiences during casting and the few voices that had clouded my judgment about sharing what I wanted to do. They all confirmed what I already knew, which is that it is better to get clarity straight from them, rather than to make assumptions based on the words of others.

Why didn't I just do this from the beginning, instead of trying to craft this alone? Why didn't I ask for help and get everyone on board with my vision, which is what I normally do? They even told me that I was the first choice after the audition process because I had asked so many real questions. They knew I would genuinely help someone once we started filming.

As I write this, we are in the middle of shooting season 3 in Kansas City, Missouri. I'm excited to say that this time around, I'm not making any photo albums or planning any random events. Ninety percent of what I'm doing during this season is clearly about helping people reach an emotional breakthrough so that the changes that my brothers—Bobby, Jonathan, Antoni, and Tan— make on the outside will stick around long after we are gone.

Any time I feel a little pushback about what my job is, I stay secure in the fact that I know I'm here to help people have emotional breakthroughs. I stay steadfast in the fact that I have gotten the support of the network, the executives, and the creators of the show to go forward and be the person who fixes the inside. I have also found an audience who loves the fact that I am always about positivity, bringing out the best in people, and helping them to grow.

I feel so aligned in my life right now. Part of that is because I listened to my gut and followed my heart in crafting what I wanted my role as the culture expert to be. The slogan for the second season of *Queer Eye* was "I'm not crying, you're crying." As I walk by billboards or see digital ads with that campaign slogan, I feel an extreme sense of pride.

Queer Eye is a group effort, and we all play major and equal roles in its success. Through our show, people are learning how to have hard conversations with themselves so that they can have hard conversations with others. I'm proud that I'm a big part of what people experience when they watch *Queer Eye*—and that I do it without having to compromise who I am. We're giving people a full makeover: changing their outsides *and* their insides to get them to their most confident, happiest, and best selves possible.

I am so excited for people to see seasons 3 and 4, and all those that come in the future. I am just getting started helping people across the globe get to the roots of their issues so they can begin to grow. As I go forward with my own podcast, *Karamo*, in which people can call in to get advice from me on hard topics—and eventually, I hope, my own daytime talk show—I know I have the talent for helping people grow emotionally so they can live their best lives. No matter what their future has in store for them, I couldn't be more grateful that I've been a part of their journeys.

conclusion

As I travel around the country, I notice that people aren't communicating when it comes to politics, race, or gender. Instead, they're talking past one another. It hurts my heart, because we aren't hearing one another. The world is in conflict. As I type these words, I'm more certain than ever that we all need to reach out to one another and connect more.

The status quo can no longer be "us versus them." It should be "us versus injustice," "us versus hatred," "us versus bigotry." We need to remove the lens that's causing us to see the world in black and white. There is an emotional gray area that connects us all.

I believe that we can and will get better as a community and as a nation. There is a real way forward through empathetic listening. Empathetic listening is so important, because if all we do is talk, then we will never hear the other person. When we hear the other person, we come to realize that we *all* want joy and love, and to be free of fears and anxieties. We realize that the conflicts facing us internally and those facing us externally are more universal than we think. It's when we support one another and respond to life's conflicts with emotional awareness that we find growth and connection.

I talk to people every day who know me from *Queer Eye* or on social media. (Hey, friends!) They tell me how uncertain they feel in this or that situation, and how opening up and being open to other people's views has aided them in living a better life. One of the things I hear a lot is that they wish they had a mini version of me in their pocket to help them feel better and solve the issues they're having in their lives.

Being open starts within ourselves: forgiving ourselves for our perceived shortcomings, for the traumas of our past, for not always making the best choices for ourselves and others. For not always responding to conflict in a healthy way.

This is something that we can start in our neighborhoods. For example, saying a genuine hello to that neighbor you may have negative feelings about because of their politics could lead to a transformative conversation. Start a dialogue and listen. Really give them an opportunity to be heard and seen. Do it without feeling the need to chime in until they're through. If they say something that doesn't sit well with you, still give them the same respect and courtesy you would want from them.

Listen, friends: we have to start talking.

From my experience talking to people all over the country—in airports, in cafés, on the train—I've come to the conclusion that we are all tired of the anger and hatred we harbor toward one another. Over the years, we have drifted further and further apart. Our schedules have become busier and busier. Our attention is more focused on our smartphones and social media feeds than on one another. I like to say to people, "Look up!" when they're walking toward me and staring at their phone. I remember Ian and I were strolling down the street in Atlanta. I said, "Look up!" to a woman who was about to bump into us. When she did, I saw her face and she saw mine. We saw each other. We need to see one another again.

We need to be kind to one another. Acts of kindness ripple across the world. When we are selflessly kind to someone, it not only makes them feel good but makes us feel good, too. Over the years, I've gotten to a place where when I ask someone how they're doing, I mean it. Or when I compliment them, it comes from a genuine place. By people's reactions, I can tell that they aren't used to it—but it changes their mood and brightens their day. It does the same thing for me.

Someday, I hope to host my own talk show where I can meet people from all over the country and bring them together. I want to help them—and us—understand our differences and similarities, and by doing so, come closer. Who knows where that could lead? Maybe I'll run for office and continue to be a voice for a greater good. Anything is possible!

I can't know what the future will hold. What I do know is that we all have the ability to effect change within ourselves and outwardly. We can reach out to one another and find ways to move the needle on success and love. Remember that growth starts at the root.

I look forward to meeting you one day in person. I'm excited to be with you on this journey of healing and growth.

acknowledgments

This book could never have happened without the support and enthusiasm of Esther Newberg, Heather Karpas, Tyler Kross, and everyone at ICM Partners.

I want to thank my mom, Charmaine; my sisters Nedra and Kamilah; my sons, Jason and Christian; my sons' mother, Stephanie; my best friends Ray and Tre; my friend Edgardo; and my fiancé, Ian, for allowing me to tell my story, but also to share a bit of yours. I love you so much!

I want to thank my *Queer Eye* castmates Bobby, Tan, Jonathan, and Antoni for being on this crazy journey with me. No matter what, I love you all.

I am so grateful to my team at Gallery Books. Huge thanks to Jen Bergstrom, Jen Long, Aimee Bell, Jeremie Ruby-Strauss, Molly Gregory, Brita Lundberg, Monica Oluwek, John Paul Jones, Erica Ferguson, Davina Mock-Maniscalco, John Vairo, Lisa Litwack, Jessica Roth, Jen Robinson, Abby Zidle, Diana Velasquez, Mackenzie Hickey, and Anabel Jimenez.

I want to thank my fabulous and fierce lawyer Emily Downs for always being in my corner. And I want to thank Jancee, my co-author, whose patience and passion for this memoir has allowed me to create something magical.

To all my friends around the world . . . the ones I know personally or those who follow my career: it's because of your desire to grow emotionally and mentally that there is a space for me in this crazy world we call entertainment. I'm glad to hear you and see you each day. You motivate me more than you know.

Most important, I must acknowledge my father, Henry "Lucky" Brown. You were a good father and good man who made many mistakes. I loved you as a child and I love you now as an adult. I forgive you for your past because I know you were on your journey of growth. You taught me more than you know and put me on the path I am on. You were my hero. I pray one day you will see the man you raised and love me unconditionally for who I am: a proud black, gay, Christian man who is raising your two amazing grandsons, marrying a special man, and working to change the world. Your goal was to raise an educated rebel, and here I am. I pray we can see each other, forgive each other, and grow together one day. Your journey is going to inspire people to correct their behavior and guide others to a "luckier" day. I guess we both lived up to our names.

Flaws and all . . . we are all designed perfectly.

about the author

Karamo Brown, the culture expert on Netflix's *Queer Eye*, is a former social worker and psychotherapist who was first introduced to audiences on MTV's *The Real World* in 2004 and then continued to build their trust as a host on *Dr. Drew Live*, *HuffPost Live*, and *Access Hollywood Live*. He also founded 6in10, an organization that provides mental health support and education to the LGBTQ+ community. He lives in Los Angeles with his fiancé and two sons.